Footprint I andbook

This is
Barbados

Tourism and Barbados go together like rum and coke or flying fish and chips. You can pay thousands of dollars to be truly cosseted along with music moguls and supermodels, or you can cater for yourself and go shopping with Bajans. The west coast, commonly referred to as the Platinum Coast, is the place to be seen.

The south is for beach life, nightlife, fun and games, the package-holiday end of the market with a cheerful, relaxed atmosphere and the best sand. The east is wild and untamed, a world apart, where the Atlantic crashes into cliffs, eroding the coastline and creating beaches of a rare beauty. Head to the hills inland to explore relics of colonial days such as plantation houses, signal towers, tropical gardens, museums and rum distilleries.

Of all the islands in the eastern Caribbean, Barbados is unique in that it remained British throughout its colonial history, without being passed from one European master to another. The island is divided into 11 parishes named after 10 saints, Christ Church being the 11th. Many of the parish churches are impressive buildings.

Towns have the charming English seaside resort names of Hastings, Brighton or Dover and the island was often referred to as Little England, not always as a compliment. Since independence in 1966 the country has moved closer in cultural terms to North America while also pursuing its African roots. Drum music, banned by colonial masters to prevent slave rebellions, and 'tuk' bands are an essential part of carnival processions. Calypso, soca and pan music are a centrepiece of Crop Over, the boisterous festival celebrating the end of the sugar harvest. However, some habits die hard. You can still go to a polo match and be offered tea and cucumber sandwiches, or watch Sunday cricket on the village green. A Test Match at the Kensington Oval, though, is a sight to behold – an example of how an English sport has been turned into pure Afro-Caribbean pageantry

Lizzie Williams

Best of
Barbados

❶ The Garrison Historic Area

If you can tear yourself away from the beach, Bridgetown's Garrison Historic Area is well worth a visit. Dating back to 1650, it's believed to be the most authentic and complete British garrison in the world and was recognized by UNESCO in 2011 for its architectural significance. Watch the changing of the guard, walk through the tunnels or take a tour to find out what George Washington thought about Barbados. Page 38.

❷ Welchman Hall Gully

This is an opportunity to see Barbados' fauna and flora in their natural state; tucked into a ravine, it's a quiet and peaceful haven shaded by tall trees where green monkeys hang out in the canopy while centipedes, frogs and other creatures can be spotted on the forest floor. From the top of the steps there is a wonderful view over much of the island. Page 52.

❸ Flower Forest Botanical Gardens

The best of the island's diverse flora is preserved in this lush tropical forest. Wander among spectacular trees and exotic flowers of all shapes and colours up to the top of the mountain for panoramic views over the wild east coast. It's a wonderfully tranquil place and an oasis of cool on a hot day. Page 53.

❹ St Nicholas Abbey

This plantation is one of only three genuine Jacobean mansions in the western hemisphere and it oozes old-world charm. With a small working rum distillery, the beautiful house and lush gardens provide a fascinating insight into the history of the sugar trade. Watch the sugar cane being crushed using steam power, taste the end product and don't forget to take home a personally engraved bottle of rum. Page 60.

❺ Bathsheba

A jagged arc of golden sand fringed with palm trees, Bathsheba is one of the most stunning beaches in Barbados. Located on the island's undeveloped east coast, it's a wild and windswept place with huge boulders jutting out of the sea. It's not safe for swimming but the huge Atlantic rollers are renowned as a surfers' heaven where young Bajans hone their skills on their boards. Page 65.

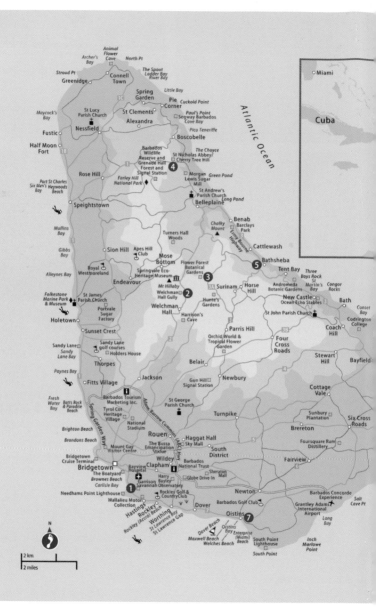

Miami

Cuba

Atlantic Ocean

Animal
Flower
Cave
Archer's
Bay
North Pt
Stroud Pt
The Spout
Ladder Bay
River Bay
Connell
Town
Greenidge
Little Bay
Spring
Garden
Cuckold Point
Pie
Corner
St Lucy
Parish Church
St Clements
Paul's Point
Segway Barbados
Cove Bay
Maycock's
Bay
Nessfield
Alexandra
Pico Teneriffe
Fustic
Boscobelle
Half Moon
Fort
Barbados
Wildlife
Reserve and
Grenade Hall
Forest and
Signal Station
The Choyce
St Nicholas Abbey/
Cherry Tree Hill
Rose Hill
Port St Charles
Six Men's Bay Heywoods
Beach
Morgan
Lewis Sugar
Mill
Green Pond
Farley Hill
National Park
Speightstown
St Andrew's
Parish Church
Belleplaine
Long Pond
Mullins
Bay
Turners Hall
Woods
Chalky
Mount
Benab
Barclays
Park
Gibbs
Bay
Sion Hill
Apes Hill
Club
Cattlewash
Alleynes Bay
Mose
Bottom
Flower Forest
Botanical
Gardens
Bathsheba
Tent Bay
Three
Boys Rock
Royal
Westmoreland
Springvale Eco-
Heritage Museum
Endeavour
St Martin's
Bay
Congor
Rocks
Folkestone Marine Park
& Museum
St James
Parish Church
Mt Hillaby
Welchman
Hall Gully
Surinam
Horse
Hill
Andromeda
Botanic Gardens
New Castle
Bath
Holetown
Portvale
Sugar
Factory
Welchman
Hall
Hunte's
Gardens
Ocean Echo Stables
Conset
Bay
Sunset Crest
Harrison's
Cave
Parris Hill
St John Parish Church
Coach
Hill
Codrington
College
Sandy Lane
Sandy Lane
golf courses
Holders House
Orchid World &
Tropical Flower
Garden
Four
Cross
Roads
Stewart
Hill
Bayfield
Thorpes
Belair
Newbury
Paynes Bay
Jackson
Gun Hill
Signal Station
Cottage
Vale
Fitts Village
Barbados Tourism
Marketing Inc.
Tyrol Cot
Heritage
Village
St George
Parish Church
Turnpike
Sunbury
Plantation
Six Cross
Roads
Fresh
Water
Bay
Batts Rock
& Paradise
Beach
National
Stadium
Brereton
Brighton Beach
The Bussa
Emancipation Statue
Rouen
Haggat Hall
Sky Mall
South
District
Wildey
Foursquare Rum
Distillery
Fairview
Brandons Beach
Mount Gay
Visitor Centre
Clapham
Barbados
National Trust
Bridgetown Cruise Terminal
The Boatyard
Brownes Beach
Carlisle Bay
Bayview
Hospital
Garrison
Savannah Observatory
Sheraton
Mall
Globe Drive-In
Needhams Point Lighthouse
Harry
Bayley
Observatory
Newton
Barbados Concorde
Experience
Hastings
Mallalieu Motor
Collection
Rockley
Rockley (Accra) Beach
Worthing
Rockley Golf &
Country Club
Dover
Barbados Golf Club
Grantley Adams
International Airport
Salt
Cave Pt
St Lawrence Bay
St Lawrence Gap
Oistins
Long
Bay
Dover Beach
Oistins
Bay
Enterprise
(Miami)
Beach
South Point
Lighthouse
Inch
Marlowe
Point
Maxwell Beach
Welches Beach
South Point

N

2 km
2 miles

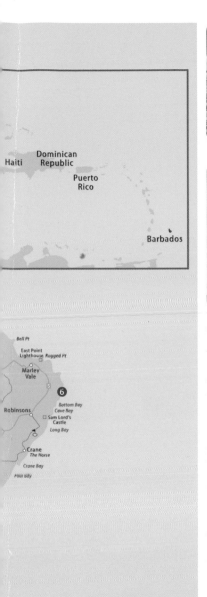

❻ Bottom Bay

Tucked away on the south coast, Bottom Bay is the ultimate tropical beach: a wide expanse of soft pink sand backed with swaying coconut palms and gently lapped by turquoise water. From the high coral cliffs behind the beach there's a panoramic view of the south coast and, if you're lucky, you might spot a turtle or a whale offshore. Page 72.

❼ Oistins Friday Fish Fry

Friday night in Oistins is the island's biggest party. Join the locals as they gather at the bustling seaside fish market with live entertainment, street vendors, crafts and traditional food. Jostle with the crowds and dance the night away with some barbecued flying fish in one hand and a potent rum punch in the other. Page 76.

Snorkelling, Bridgetown

Route planner

putting it all together

Many holidaymakers to the Caribbean only venture out of their all-inclusive resorts on the occasional organized excursion, but, thanks to excellent public transport, good roads and short distances, Barbados is very easy to explore independently. It can take less than an hour to travel from one coast to the next; just a few hours to drive around the entire island, stopping in at one or two tourist attractions and for a leisurely lunch on the way; and, on the highly developed west and south coasts, it's no more than a short walk or bus ride to get to another beach, restaurant or shopping mall. Think of Barbados in five parts. Firstly, there's **Bridgetown** and its environs; while the island's capital is not especially big or appealing, there's good shopping and the **Garrison Historic Area** is interesting to wander around. Secondly, there's the upmarket **west coast**, where the narrow but pretty beaches are lapped by calm waters and lined with luxurious hotels and villas and some superb waterside restaurants. Thirdly, there's the heavily developed **south coast** where the beaches are wider and the sand whiter, and, while the sea is sometimes too rough for safe swimming, the family-friendly resorts have swimming pools and plenty of other amenities for some fun in the sun. Fourthly is the unspoiled, wild, wave-pummelled **east coast**, which has just a few places to stay and eat but makes for scenic driving and hiking with tremendous Atlantic views. Lastly is the island's rolling interior, which has a variety of attractions among the sugarcane fields, from plantation houses and rum distilleries to intriguing caves and beautiful flowering botanical gardens.

Best beaches
Paynes Bay Beach, page 46
Bathsheba Beach, page 65
Bottom Bay, page 72
Crane Beach, page 73
Dover Beach, page 77

One to two weeks

If you have only a week to spend on the island, you probably won't want to do much except relax. Take advantage of the beach with a sun lounger, umbrella and rum punch – at your hotel or at one of the many good beach bars. Take a boat trip, go snorkelling with the turtles or dive one of the many colonial-era wrecks littering the seabed. Then in the evening spoil yourself at the plush places

Located in the Atlantic Ocean, 483 km north of Venezuela in South America, Barbados is the easternmost island of the Lesser Antilles in the West Indies, and is about 100 km east of the Windward Islands arc and the Caribbean Sea. The island, which is 34 km long, 23 km at its widest point and covers an area of 430 sq km is sometimes referred to as pear-shaped. The 97-km-long coastline features fine beaches and narrow coastal plains with several steep inland cliffs or ridges. The highest point is Mount Hillaby (337 m) in the north-central area; not a peaked mountain, but an extended ridge about 4 km long. Relatively flat compared to its volcanic neighbours, about 85% of the island is covered by a cap of coral limestone underlain by sedimentary rock up to 600,000 years old. This means that most of the rainwater runs through caves in the limestone – one of these, Harrison's Cave, has been developed as a tourist attraction – and runs off underground and through steep-sided gullies. The island's water supply is pumped up from the limestone and, as it's filtered, is generally very good for drinking. In the Scotland District in the northeast, the coral limestone has been eroded and older, softer rocks are exposed; the area is made up of clay, sandstone and shale with jutting rocky spikes and ridges. With the exception of the Constitution River in Bridgetown, the island's other three rivers (the Long Pond River and Bruce Vale River in St Andrew, and Joe's River in St Joseph) are in the Scotland District, and have cut deep, steep-sided valleys. Prior to being settled in 1627, Barbados was covered in dense tropical rainforest, but almost all of this was cut down to make way for sugar plantations and later developement. Only two examples of this forest remain: Turner's Hall Woods and Joe's River Rain Forest. Barbados was first divided into six parishes in 1629 and later, in 1645, was divided into the present 11 parishes: St Lucy, St Peter, St James, St Thomas, Christ Church, St Michael, St Joseph, St Andrew, St John, St George and St Philip.

with seafront dining on the west or **Platinum Coast** or, if you are on the south coast, wander down to **St Lawrence Gap**, the 'happening' place for restaurants and bars. Other popular options are the dinner and beach party on Mondays and Wednesdays at **Harbour Lights**, and **Oistins Fish Fry** on Fridays with calypso, soca and live music. It's well worth dragging yourself away from the sand to explore the island and put Barbados' history as a British colony into perspective. Hop on a bus to **Bridgetown** one day and spend a morning sightseeing around the **Garrison Historic Area** and shopping along **Broad Street**, with perhaps lunch at a restaurant overlooking the boats in the **Careenage** or some rum tasting at the **Mount Gay Visitor Centre**.

Two weeks or more

If you have two weeks on Barbados why not move around a bit? Spend a few days on the south coast first to wind down and enjoy the beach and the nightlife around **St Lawrence Gap**. Then, when the jet lag is behind you and if you can splurge, move up to another resort or plush hotel on the west coast to enjoy some luxury. Finally, stay in a guesthouse on the east coast for a different view of the island: the pounding Atlantic creates a very scenic and wild string of beaches. Hire a car for part of your holiday and tour the island; you can drive all round Barbados in five hours, but temptation will get in your way and you'll stop frequently. You'll also probably get lost, as road signs are not a big feature and the island is criss-crossed with hundreds of little twisty roads through villages. A day could be spent at **Bathsheba**, hiking along the old coastal railway, strolling around **Andromeda Botanic Gardens** or lolling about in rock pools. A northern tour could take in **Speightstown**, the **Animal Flower Cave**, **Farley Hill**, the **Barbados Wildlife Reserve** and **Grenade Hall Forest** and **Signal Station**, **St Nicholas Abbey** and the **Morgan Lewis Sugar Mill**. A day in the middle of the island could encompass the **Harrison's Cave**, the **Flower Forest Botanical Gardens**, **Orchid World & Tropical Flower Garden**, **Gun Hill Signal Station** and **Sunbury Plantation House**.

When to go

… and when not to

Climate

Any time of year is holiday time in Barbados but some months are better than others, depending on what you want to do. The climate is tropical, but rarely excessively hot because of the trade winds. Temperatures vary between 21°C and 35°C, the coolest and driest time being December-May, and a wet and hotter season June-November. Rain is usually heavy when it comes but, because of its easterly position in the Caribbean, Barbados has rarely been hit by hurricanes.

Festivals

If you want a carnival atmosphere then time your visit for **Crop Over**, from late June-to early August – the main carnival celebrations take place the first weekend of August; book flights, accommodation and car hire in plenty of time for this long weekend as everything is very busy with both Barbadians, returning family and friends and visiting tourists. Other musical events worth aiming for are the **Holders Season** in March and the **Celtic Festival** in May with lots of music, dance and sports. Cricket lovers should try to take in a **Test Match** or a regional competition to see top international players at the Kensington Oval, but there are cricket festivals at other times of the year and of course matches every Sunday in villages around the island. In terms of price, hotel and villa rates are

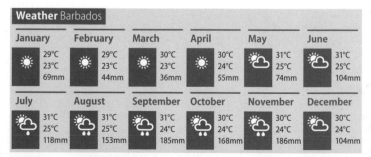

Weather Barbados					
January 29°C 23°C 69mm	**February** 29°C 23°C 44mm	**March** 30°C 23°C 36mm	**April** 30°C 24°C 55mm	**May** 31°C 25°C 74mm	**June** 31°C 25°C 104mm
July 31°C 25°C 118mm	**August** 31°C 25°C 153mm	**September** 31°C 24°C 185mm	**October** 30°C 24°C 168mm	**November** 30°C 24°C 186mm	**December** 30°C 24°C 104mm

much higher from mid-December to April than at other times of year (especially over Christmas/New Year and Easter, when additional premiums are often charged), while in the quietest and wettest months of September and October, some hotels, restaurants and bars close altogether.

For a diary of events and festivals see www.whatsoninbarbados.com. For public holidays, see page 115.

January

Barbados Horticultural Society (BHS) Annual Flower & Garden Show

BHS Headquarters, Balls Plantation, Christ Church, T428 5889, www.horticulture barbados.com. Held on the last weekend in January, there are lovely floral exhibits from societies affiliated to the BHS including the Barbados Flower Arranging Society, Bonsai Barbados, Barbados Orchid Society and the Barbados Cactus and Succulent Society, as well as craft, tea and food stalls.

Naniki Barbados Music Festival *T433 1351, www.nanikicaribbeanjazzsafari.com.* Usually the second weekend in January, this Caribbean-wide R&B, jazz, reggae and calypso festival organizes a series of concerts showcasing Barbadian, regional and international talent with the main venues being Frank Collymore Hall in Bridgetown and Holders on the west coast.

February

Holetown Festival *www.holetown festivalbarbados.org.* The week-long festival begins in mid-February and commemorates the first settlers' landing in February 1627. There are parades with floats during the day, all well organized and restrained, nothing outrageous. The Mallalieu Motor Collection lends its vintage cars, one of which carries Miss

Best gardens
Orchid World and Tropical Flower Garden, page 44
Flower Forest Botanical Gardens, page 53
Hunte's Gardens, page 54
St Nicholas Abbey, page 60
Andromeda Botanic Gardens, page 66

Holetown; a few kids march in costume, there are one or two masked performers, and stalls are set up, selling food, Banks beer and crafts. One of the most popular events is the Police Tattoo, an outdoor night show featuring the men and women of the Royal Barbados Police Force. The Police Force band play on a stage on the beach and the mounted troop, canine unit and motorcycle unit are usually on display. This is Little England par excellence.

March

Holders Season *Holders Hill, St James, T432 6385, www.holdersseason.com.* The major music, opera, drama, comedy and cabaret festival in the Caribbean. International artistes flock to perform here in front of an enthusiastic audience of locals and visitors, but not all the talent is imported. The setting is unbelievably romantic, in the garden of the 17th-century Holders House overlooking a golf course and polo field, with thousands

ON THE ROAD
Flourishing gardens

In May 2016, Barbados exhibited for the 28th consecutive year at the UK's prestigious Royal Horticultural Society's annual Chelsea Flower Show and yet again won a Gold Medal. This was Gold Medal number 17 among many other Highly Commendable appearances at the show which have also included Silver Gilt and Silver medals. The beautiful and creative floral displays are organized by the Barbados Horticultural Society (BHS; T428 5889, www.horticulturebarbados.com), which has been in existence since 1927. A good part of any success at Chelsea comes from mastering the art of transporting flowers and foliage, and each year team Barbados individually wraps every petal, leaf and stem before boxing them up and dispatching them across the Atlantic to London with British Airways.

In addition to the spectacular gardens open to the public on Barbados, such as Orchid World and Tropical Flower Garden, Hunte's Gardens, Flower Forest Botanical Gardens and Andromeda Botanic Gardens, Barbados has numerous private gardens which are lovingly tended by their owners. Check the events page on the website of the BHS for details of its Open Garden Programme when private gardens can be visited, usually Sundays 1400-1800 from January to March (there is a small entry fee, tea and refreshments). On the last weekend in January, the BHS host their Annual Flower and Garden Show at their headquarters at Balls Plantation in Christ Church (once an 18th-century sugar estate), where it has 5 ha (12 acres) of landscaped gardens.

of fairy lights twinkling in the palm trees and among the shrubs. Take a picnic and a bottle of bubbly; it's a great social occasion. Don't forget your umbrella and insect repellent.

Oistins Fish Festival *Bay Gardens, Oistins, Christ Church, T426 6870, www. oistinsfestival.org.* Held at Easter to celebrate the signing of the Charter of Barbados and the history of this fishing town. There are three days of competitions, parades and demonstrations of fishing skills. Fish-boning is the major competition, the winner being the Queen of the Festival.

There are also boat races, the greasy pole and a big street party with live music which goes on until late at night – and of course, lots of fried fish and fish cakes. On Easter Sunday there is a **Gospel Festival**. A very popular event attracting thousands of people.

April
Barbados International Fishing Tournament *Port St Charles, St Peter, www.barbadosgamefishing.com.* Held in mid-April, this, one of the premier fishing events in the southern Caribbean, attracts participants from across the region and internationally for five days of competition. Apart from the fishing, there's much dockside activity and in the evenings people gather to witness the boats arriving with their catch and join in the cocktail parties, a fashion show, wine-tasting, live bands, a pig-roast and fish fry.

Barbados Reggae Festival *T257 4356, www.thebarbadosreggaefestival.com.* Held in the third week of April and featuring top-quality local, regional and international reggae acts with a beach party, cruise parties, and the very popular Reggae on the Hill open-air concert at Farley Hill National Park.

May

Barbados Celtic Festival *www.barbados celticfestival.com.* Held over four days at the end of May on the South Coast Boardwalk, this is rather an unusual festival to be celebrated in the Caribbean, but Barbados attracts Celtic people from around the world for their annual *gymanfa-ganu* and other events including folk music, street theatre, ceilidhs and Celtic chefs. The main event is a parade of pipes and drums in Bridgetown on the Saturday morning.

Gospelfest, *www.barbadosgospelfest.com.* Held over Whitsun, the last weekend in May, this international festival attracts gospel singers from the USA, UK and all over the Caribbean. Concerts are held at various locations including Farley Hill National Park.

August

Banks International Hockey Festival *www.barbadoshockey.org.* Hockey is very popular in Barbados and this is the largest field hockey event in the region, with teams coming from all over the world to participate. Held at Sir Garfield Sobers Sports Complex in late August,

matches take place during the day and are followed by beach parties, fêtes, party cruises and clubbing.

November

Barbados Food and Rum Festival Takes place over five days in late November and includes hotels for gourmet suppers with cooking demonstrations by eminent chefs, and the 'Taste of the Exotic', the main rum-tasting event held at the Barbados Concorde Experience. There are more tastings with a polo match at Holders.

Independence Day Although the actual day is 30 November, there are several events during the month commemorating Barbados' independence from Britain in 1966, including a parade on the Savannah.

National Independence Festival of Creative Arts (NIFCA) *Contact the National Cultural Foundation, T417 6610, www.ncf.bb.* Plays, concerts and exhibitions in the four weeks before Independence Day on 30 November. Competitors work their way up through parish heats to reach the finals at the Frank Collymore Hall in Bridgetown.

December

Classical/Pops Festival *Apes Hill Club, St James, www.classicalpops.com.* Held on the second Friday and Saturday in December on an outdoor stage at the Apes Hill Golf and Country Club, featuring orchestral musicians in collaboration with pop stars, Broadway performers and opera divas.

ON THE ROAD
Crop Over

The origins of Crop Over, the main festival in Barbados, can be traced back to the 1780s when Barbados was one of the world's largest producers of sugar. For about 30 years around the mid-20th century it went uncelebrated, but was resurrected for tourist purposes in 1974. Since then it has grown into a major celebration of Barbadian culture enjoyed by all, and nobody gets much work done during the six weeks that it lasts – from late June when the sugar cane harvest ends until the first Monday in August: the **Grand Kadooment**. Parades and calypso competitions lead up to this finale, although there are calypso 'tents' and other events during the weeks beforehand.

The celebrations begin with the ceremonial delivery of the last canes on a brightly coloured dray cart pulled by mules, which are blessed. There is a toast to the sugar workers and the crowning of the King and Queen of the crop (the champion cutter-pilers). Weekly calypso tent shows showcase the latest songs with performances by entertainers and comedians as well as calypsonians. Parties, also known as fêtes or bashments, start with after-work liming, hotting up around midnight and going on until daybreak. The **Junior Kadooment Parade** and **Junior Calypso Monarch Competition** give children a chance to have their own carnival and play 'mas'.

Things start to hot up big time on the Friday night preceding the Grand Kadooment with the **Pic-O-De-Crop** semi-finals and **Party Monarch Calypso Competition**. From a line-up of 18, seven competitors are selected to go forward to the finals to compete against the reigning Calypso Monarch. This is held on the Ermy Bourne Highway on the east coast and is combined with the Party Monarch Calypso Competition, so a great day is had by all with picnics, music and liming overlooking the Atlantic surf.

Following the selection of the King of Pic-O-De-Crop Calypso there is **Fore-Day Morning Jump Up**, an event borrowed from Trinidad's carnival, which is held in the early hours of the Saturday morning. It starts in Bridgetown and heads out to Spring Garden Highway; wear old clothes as a lot of oils and paints get liberally smeared around and it ends with a sunrise beach party. On Sunday night **Cohobblopot** is when the kings and queens of the costume bands show off their creations and compete for prizes and the titles of King and Queen of the Festival. On the Monday, the **Grand Kadooment** is the finale of the carnival, when there is a procession of costume bands through the streets, again along Spring Garden Highway, accompanied by trucks of deafening sound systems and fuelled by alcohol. Your eyes will be blasted with colour by costumed dancers, stilt walkers and masqueraders, your ears blasted with sound by tuk bands, calypso, ringbang and steel pan, and your gut blasted by rum, beer, sun, adrenalin and lack of sleep. After the parade the party continues well into the night on Brighton Beach with more revelry, music, food and fireworks.

Details and dates of all events are published on the Barbados Crop Over Festival Facebook page, as well as on the website of Barbados Tourism Marketing Inc (BTMI), www.visitbarbados.org.

What to do

from cricket, golf and polo to diving and sailing

Cricket

Cricket is king in Barbados and everybody has an opinion on the state of the game as well as the latest results. Going to watch a cricket match is an entertaining cultural experience and well worth doing, even if you don't understand the game. Village cricket is played all over the island at weekends; a match here is nothing if not a social occasion. Cricket lovers should try to arrange their visit to coincide with a Test Match or a One Day International at the Kensington Oval (see page 94). No sedate Sunday afternoon crowd this – the atmosphere is electric, with DJ music, constant whistling, horn-blowing, cheering and banter. At lunch there are food stalls outside where you can pick up a burger, roti or Bajan stew, buy a T-shirt and West Indies hat and drink a few Banks beers. The biggest crowds come for the matches against England, with touring teams tagging along, but cricket tourists come from as far afield as Australia or South Africa.

Diving and snorkelling

Barbados is surrounded by an inner reef and an outer barrier reef. On the west coast the inner reef is within swimming distance for snorkelling or learning to dive, while the outer reef is a short boat ride away and the water is deeper. Here you can see barracuda, king fish, moray eels, turtles and squid as well as some fine black coral, barrel sponges and sea fans. The underwater landscape may not be as pristine as some other islands, but there are some excellent wrecks worth exploring and Carlisle Bay is littered with bottles, cannon balls, anchors and small items such as buckles and buttons after many centuries of visiting ships 'losing' things overboard or sinking. There are 200 reported wrecks in Carlisle Bay, but another popular dive site is the SS Stavronikita in the Folkestone Marine Park, one of the best diving wrecks in the Caribbean. See page 51. Water temperatures are usually about 25°C in winter and 28°C in summer, with visibility of 15-30 m. A highlight for snorkellers is to swim with the turtles – at Sandy Bay you can see them close to the beach; otherwise Paynes Bay and Folkestone Marine Park offer plenty of opportunity for those prepared to swim out a distance to find them. A number of tour operators run boat excursions to sites frequented by turtles.

Golf

Many keen golfers come to Barbados just to play golf and there are enough courses

ON THE ROAD
Open House Programme

On Saturdays and some Wednesdays between January and March, the Barbados National Trust (T426 2421, www.barbadosnationaltrust.org, see also page 80) organizes public visits to some of the island's most historic and elegant homes as part of the Open House Programme. They could be anything from a grand 17th-century plantation house on a former sugar estate to a colonial seaside villa or historic church, and often they are beautifully decorated with antiques and sit in magnificent grounds. A garden party atmosphere prevails at these events, with fresh juices, rum punch, tea and snacks served on the lawns. Books on Barbados and the Caribbean are available for purchase, and artists and craftspeople sell their goods. Cost is B$35, children (12-17) B$15, under 12s free. You can get the schedules and directions off the website and signs are erected to help visitors find the houses. No booking is required; arrive at 1400 for a tour followed by a lecture at 1515 and tea at about 1545.

to keep anyone busy for a while, with several 18-hole and nine-hole courses, from the public Barbados Golf Club to the more exclusive Sandy Lane (where Tiger Woods got married). The **RBC Golf Classic** is held in November; the **Barbados Open** in August; the **Sir Garfield Sobers Festival of Golf Championships** in May and other competitions throughout the year. The **Barbados Golf Association** publishes a schedule of events, www.barbadosgolfassociation.com. See page 96 for details of the courses.

Hiking

The most beautiful part of the island is the Scotland District on the east coast. There is also some fine country along the St Lucy coast in the north and on the southeast coast. There is a particularly good hiking route along the old railway track, from Bath to Bathsheba and on to Cattlewash. The Barbados National Trust organizes very enjoyable and sociable three-hour guided hikes every Sunday to various locations; see page 96.

Horse racing

Horse racing dates back to colonial days when planters challenged each other to races. Later the cavalry officers of the British army joined in and by 1840 there were regular race days at the Garrison. Regular races are still held there, the biggest of which is the **Sandy Lane Barbados Gold Cup** held in March, which features horses from neighbouring islands. Again, this is something of a social occasion, with parties, parades and concerts. The Royal Barbados Mounted Police band leads a parade of dancers, tumblers and stiltmen in carnival fashion. See box, page 39.

Polo

An unusual spectator sport for a Caribbean island is polo, which appears to have been dropped in from the Home Counties and is followed avidly by mostly white expats. It has been played since cavalry officers introduced the game in the 19th century and the Polo Club was formed in 1884. Matches were originally played at the Garrison Savannah, where ponies were often reject race horses, but there are now several polo fields on the island and its popularity has steadily risen. The season runs from just after Christmas until May, with lots of visiting teams from overseas coming to compete. See page 97.

Sailing

Sailing can be a bit choppy along the south coast to Oistins and most races head up the west coast where the waters are calmer. In January there is the **Mount Gay Round Barbados Race**, www.mountgayrumround barbadosrace.com, while the three-day **May Regatta** is the main event of the year. Carlisle Bay is the main anchorage and focal point for the sailing fraternity.

There are lots of motor and sailing boats available for charter by the week, day or for shorter periods. Cruises up the west side of the island with stops for snorkelling and swimming with turtles are very popular, whether for lunch or sunset watching. The larger catamarans can be cheaper than the smaller ones but they are often packed to the gunnels and can feel crowded. On a less busy day they are enjoyable, but it is difficult to find out how booked each cruise is likely to be. When cruise ships are in port, the catamarans are very busy with 50-100 guests on board. Those boats that limit numbers are likely to be more friendly and relaxed with better service. See page 97.

Surfing

The best surfing is on the east coast at the Soup Bowl, Bathsheba, which has the most consistent break. The best time is August-November when you get perfect barrelling waves. Experienced surfers also like Duppies on the north coast, where you have a long paddle out and there is a lot of current, but the waves are really big. The south coast is good for beginners and for boogie boarding, although there is a good break at Brandons, while the west coast has some good spots with easy access, often best when there are no waves on the east coast. Sandy Lane, Tropicana, Gibbs and Maycock's are all worth trying.

The Barbados international surfing championship, **Independence PRO**, is held at the Soup Bowl, Bathsheba, in November, but there are national competitions in August and September. See page 98.

Windsurfing and kitesurfing

The south coast is good for windsurfing and kitesurfing. The centre of the action for windsurfers is Silver Rock. There is a 3-km stretch of reef providing excellent waves for wave sailors and a lagoon for those who are less confident. The best place to learn to windsurf is in the Sandy Beach area inside the lagoon, while outside the reef you can sometimes get good wave sailing. On the north coast the waves can be very big at Cow Pens and Red Backs. Access is not easy as there is only a very small beach from which to launch yourself.

Kitesurfing is best done further east near the airport, at Long Beach, where the wind is side on shore. The wind is best from November to July. When the wind is light and windsurfers can't go out, then the area between Silver Sands Beach and Silver Rock Beach is good for beginners.

Improve your travel photography

Taking pictures is a highlight for many travellers, yet too often the results turn out to be disappointing. Steve Davey, author of Footprint's *Travel Photography*, sets out his top rules for coming home with pictures you can be proud of.

Before you go

Don't waste precious travelling time and do your research before you leave. Find out what festivals or events might be happening or which day the weekly market takes place, and search online image sites such as Flickr to see whether places are best shot at the beginning or end of the day, and what vantage points you should consider.

Get up early

The quality of the light will be better in the few hours after sunrise and again before sunset – especially in the tropics when the sun will be harsh and unforgiving in the middle of the day. Sometimes seeing the sunrise is a part of the whole travel experience: sleep in and you will miss more than just photographs.

Stop and think

Don't just click away without any thought. Pause for a few seconds before raising the camera and ask yourself what you are trying to show with your photograph. Think about what things you need to include in the frame to convey this meaning. Be prepared to move around your subject to get the best angle. Knowing the point of your picture is the first step to making sure that the person looking at the picture will know it too.

Compose your picture

Avoid simply dumping your subject in the centre of the frame every time you take a picture. If you compose with it to one side, then your picture can look more balanced. This will also allow you to show a significant background and make the picture more meaningful. A good rule of thumb is to place your subject or any significant detail a third of the way into the frame; facing into the frame not out of it.

This rule also works for landscapes. Compose with the horizon two-thirds of the way up the frame if the foreground is the most interesting part of the picture; one-third of the way up if the sky is more striking.

Don't get hung up with this so-called Rule of Thirds, though. Exaggerate it by pushing your subject out to the edge of the frame if it makes a more interesting picture; or if the sky is dull in a landscape, try cropping with the horizon near the very top of the frame.

Fill the frame

If you are going to focus on a detail or even a person's face in a close-up portrait, then be bold and make sure that you fill the frame. This is often a case of physically getting in close. You can use a telephoto setting on a zoom lens but this can lead to pictures looking quite flat; moving in close is a lot more fun!

Interact with people

If you want to shoot evocative portraits then it is vital to approach people and seek permission in some way, even if it is just by smiling at someone. Spend a little time with them and they are likely to relax and look less stiff and formal. Action portraits where people are doing something, or environmental portraits, where they are set against a significant background, are a good way to achieve relaxed portraits. Interacting is a good way to find out more about people and their lives, creating memories as well as photographs.

Focus carefully

Your camera can focus quicker than you, but it doesn't know which part of the picture you want to be in focus. If your camera is using the centre focus sensor then move the camera so it is over the subject and half press the button, then, holding it down, recompose the picture. This will lock the focus. Take the now correctly focused picture when you are ready.

Another technique for accurate focusing is to move the active sensor over your subject. Some cameras with touch-sensitive screens allow you to do this by simply clicking on the subject.

Leave light in the sky

Most good night photography is actually taken at dusk when there is some light and colour left in the sky; any lit portions of the picture will balance with the sky and any ambient lighting. There is only a very small window when this will happen, so get into position early, be prepared and keep shooting and reviewing the results. You can take pictures after this time, but avoid shots of tall towers in an inky black sky; crop in close on lit areas to fill the frame.

Bring it home safely

Digital images are inherently ephemeral: they can be deleted or corrupted in a heartbeat. The good news though is they can be copied just as easily. Wherever you travel, you should have a backup strategy. Cloud backups are popular, but make sure that you will have access to fast enough Wi-Fi. If you use RAW format, then you will need some sort of physical back-up. If you don't travel with a laptop or tablet, then you can buy a backup drive that will copy directly from memory cards

Available in both digital and print formats, Footprint's Travel Photography by Steve Davey covers everything you need to know about travelling with a camera, including simple post-processing. More information is available at www.footprinttravelguides.com

Where to stay

from ultra-luxurious hotels to B&Bs and everything in between

Tourism is the major industry on Barbados and there are literally hundreds of accommodation options from all-inclusive family resorts, secluded beachfront villas and full-service hotels to modestly priced apartments and guesthouses. However, overall it is an upmarket destination and visitors come here for a treat, expecting – and receiving – excellent service and high standards. Accommodation rates tend to be higher than on some of the other less popular Caribbean islands. Generally, the top hotels in the super-luxury category, costing well over US$800 per person per night, are on the west or 'Platinum' coast. Places such as **Sandy Lane**, where you can get every conceivable service and luxury, are among the world's top resorts. Mid-range, cheerful places can be found all along the south coast from about US$150-300 per room, but many of these are characterless, concrete block hotels usually booked as part of a package holiday, but they offer a wide selection of amenities and are generally good value for families. There are far fewer places to stay on the east coast, where the landscape is rugged and breezy and air conditioning is rarely needed, but many will enjoy the isolation. However, night owls will miss the entertainment as people tend to go to bed early, tired after a day of activity.

Although there are few budget options, there are apartment rentals and guesthouses, or you could opt for an apartment hotel where rooms have fully equipped kitchens, and perhaps two double beds and/or pull-out sofa beds for

Price codes

Where to stay		Restaurants	
$$$$	over US$300	$$$	over US$30
$$$	US$150-300	$$	US$15-30
$$	US$75-150	$	under US$15
$	under US$75		

Price codes refer to a standard double/twin room in high season.

Price codes refer to the cost of a two-course meal, excluding drinks or service charge.

ON THE ROAD
Chattel houses

Dating from the days of slavery, chattel houses are a distinctive part of Barbados' architectural and social heritage. These wooden houses all conformed to a basic, symmetrical plan, with a central door and a window either side, built on a foundation of loosely packed stones which allowed the air to circulate under and through the house. The steeply pitched roof would have originally been thatched but later they were all galvanized to withstand heavy winds and rain. Each chattel house was customized by its owners, who added pretty shutters, porches, jalousie windows, verandas and decorative detail such as gingerbread fretwork. The island's first chattel houses were built in the late 17th century, but they became more widespread after Emancipation in 1838. Although slaves were freed, they were still landless and therefore had to rent small plots from the plantations on which they laboured. Laws provided the labourers the right to construct modest dwellings on these plots, but with the plantation owners having the right to evict tenants at will. As a result, the key feature of all chattel houses was that they could be dismantled and moved easily, so that if a worker moved from one plantation to another he could pack up and move with 'all his goods and chattels'.

children. It may mean giving up room service and direct access to the beach, and the decor may not be up to scratch, but there are some delightful, friendly options that start at around US$80-100 per night. Costs can be brought down further by self-catering (supermarkets are well stocked with familiar brands from North America and some from the UK). Cleanliness and comfort are rarely an issue, and almost all rooms have air conditioning, TV and Wi-Fi.

High season, when rates are at their most expensive, is mid-December to mid-April. There are often discounts of around 30% in low season – September and October – but this is also the worst time for rainy weather and many hotels close altogether. Hotel VAT (7.5%) and service charge (10%) is charged across the board, usually as a single charge of 17.5%; check if this has been included in quotes. Rates are room-only, B&B or all-inclusive, meaning you get three meals a day and sometimes local drinks. Opting for an all-inclusive rate, or staying at a specifically all-inclusive resort where everything such as watersports is included, can be appealing as you know exactly what you are getting for your money (especially if you combine flights and transfers in a package). Almost all places have websites to book direct. Good listings can be found on the website of **Barbados Tourism Marketing Inc**ⓘ *www.visitbarbados.org*, and there are numerous local agents such as **Intimate Hotels of Barbados** ⓘ *www.intimatehotelsbarbados.com*. Barbados is also well represented on accommodation websites such as **www.expedia.com**, **www.booking.com**, **www.ownersdirect.co.uk** and **www.airbnb.com**.

Food
& drink

seafood, high-end gastronomy and, of course, rum punch

Just as Barbadian culture is a blend of British and African traditions, so the cuisine of Barbados is a mix of British and West African tastes and ingredients, developed over the centuries with some other flavours brought to the pot by immigrants from other nations, such as India. The need for carbohydrates to fuel slave labour and arduous work in the sugar cane fields has led to a diet based on starchy vegetables known as ground provisions, while difficulties in storing meat and fish in the tropical heat led to common use of salt meat and fish, pickles and other preserves. Sugar, the main crop of the island for generations, features heavily in both food and drink, reaching perfection in the production of rum.

Barbados is not cheap, but there are ways of making your money go further. Even on a tight budget you will need US$50 per day for food and drink. Eating where Barbadians eat for lunch, for instance, will cost you US$5-6, but lunch at a beach bar will cost two or three times that amount. Stick with local Banks beer (US$3 for 500 ml) rather than imported beers and rum is better value than wine.

Food

Fresh fish is excellent and sold at the markets in Oistins, Bridgetown and elsewhere in the late afternoon and evening, when the fishermen come in with their catch. It is a fascinating sight to watch the speed and skill with which women fillet flying fish and bag them up for sale. The main fish season is December-May, when there is less risk of stormy weather at sea. Flying fish are the national emblem and a speciality with two or three fillets to a plate, eaten with chips, breaded in a sandwich (flying fish cutter) or with an elegant sauce. Dolphin fish, also called *dorado* or *mahi mahi* on restaurant menus, and kingfish are larger steak-fish. Snapper is excellent. There is also plenty of local crab, lobster, conch (*lambi*), octopus and shrimp/prawns.

Cou-cou is a filling starchy dish made from breadfruit or corn meal with okra, peppers and hot sauce. *Jug-jug* is a Christmas speciality made from guinea corn, pigeon peas and salt meat, supposedly descended from the haggis of the poor white Scottish settlers exiled to the island after the failed Monmouth Rebellion of 1685. Pudding and souse is a huge dish of pickled breadfruit, black pudding and pork. Conkie is a corn-based dish often referred to as stew dumpling, traditionally made and sold during November, originally to celebrate the failure of Guy Fawkes' attempt to blow up the Houses of Parliament and King James I, and later to celebrate Independence from British colonial rule. Conkie contains spices, sugar, pumpkin, corn meal, coconut and sometimes raisins or cherries, all wrapped and steamed in a banana leaf, served hot.

There is a riot of tropical fruit and vegetables: unusual and often unidentifiable objects as well as more familiar items found in supermarkets in Europe and North America but with 10 times the flavour. The best bananas in the world are grown in the Caribbean; they are cheap, incredibly sweet and unlike anything you can buy at home. Many of the wonderful tropical fruits you will come across in juices or in ice cream. Don't miss the rich flavours of the soursop, the guava or the sapodilla. Mangoes in season drip off the trees and those that don't end up on your breakfast plate can be found squashed in abundance all over the roads. Caribbean oranges are often green when ripe, as there is no cold season to bring out the orange colour, and are meant for juicing not peeling. Portugals are like tangerines and easy to peel. The grapefruit originated in Barbados in the 18th century, crossing a sweet orange and a bitter citrus called a shaddock, brought from Polynesia by Captain Shaddock. Avocados are nearly always sold unripe, so wait several days before attempting to eat them. Avocados have been around since the days of the Arawaks, who also cultivated cassava and cocoa, but many vegetables have their origins in the slave trade, brought over to provide a starchy diet for the slaves. The breadfruit, a common staple rich in carbohydrates and vitamins A, B and C, was brought from the South Seas in 1793 by Captain Bligh, perhaps more famous for the mutiny on the *Bounty*. It is eaten in a variety of ways in Barbados: with tomato and onion, a cucumber and lime souse, mashed like a potato or as wafer-thin crisps. It is one of the many forms of starch popular in local cooking; others include sweet potato, yam, eddo, green banana, plantain, bakes, cassava, rice, pasta and potato. Rice usually comes mixed with pigeon peas, black-eye peas or split peas. Macaroni cheese is a popular accompaniment, and is referred to as 'pie'.

With sugar being grown on the island, Barbadians have developed a sweet tooth. It is worth trying tamarind balls, guava cheese, chocolate fudge and peanut brittle, while for dessert, coconut bread and Bajan baked custard and lemon meringue pie are firm favourites.

Drink

Barbados is a major producer of rum and you can find some excellent brands including Mount Gay, Cockspur, Malibu, Foursquare and St Nicholas Abbey. It is worth paying a bit extra for a good brand such as VSOP or Old Gold, or for the slightly sweeter Sugar Cane Brandy, unless you are going to drink it with Coca Cola, in which case anything will do. A rum and cream liqueur, *Crisma*, is popular in cocktails or on the rocks. Mount Gay produce a vanilla and a mango-flavoured rum. *Falernum* is sweet, sometimes slightly alcoholic, with a hint of vanilla and great in a rum cocktail instead of sugar syrup. If you drink in a rum shop, rum and other drinks are bought by the bottle. The smallest size is a mini, then a flask, then a full bottle. The shop will supply ice and glasses, you buy a mixer and serve yourself. 'Wine', in a rum shop, usually means sweet sherry. If you are not careful, it is drunk with ice and beer.

For non-alcoholic drinks, there is a range of refreshing fruit juices, including orange, mango, pineapple, grapefruit, lime, guava and passionfruit. *Sorrel* is a bright red drink made with hibiscus sepals and spices, and *mauby* is a bitter sweet drink made from tree bark. Both are watered down like a fruit squash and they can be refreshing with lots of ice. Banks Beer produces Bajan Light (a lager) as well as a milk stout and a non-alcoholic malt drink. Water is of excellent quality, it comes mostly from deep wells sunk into the coral limestone, but there is bottled water if you prefer.

Tip...
Try coconut water – the clear liquid inside young green coconuts, which is very refreshing. A machete is often used to cut open the nut; look for barrows and stalls piled high with coconuts and a knife-wielding vendor in markets, on the side of village streets and in car parks at the beaches.

Eating out

There are excellent restaurants on Barbados, many of gourmet standard, especially along the west coast catering to the well-heeled visitors. Some of these are in the luxury hotels such as **Sandy Lane**, but you don't have to go to a hotel for cordon bleu cuisine. Many of the chefs have been around a bit, working in high-class kitchens in London or Paris before trying a spell in the Caribbean, bringing a variety of skills to the task of preparing tropical ingredients. Eating out is not cheap, and restaurants will charge around US$12-40 for a main course, but standards are high and the settings often special; you may get an open-air waterfront table or a garden terrace, perhaps even a table on the beach. The majority of places to eat are clustered around Holetown on the west coast and St Lawrence Gap on the south coast, where you can indulge in Italian, Mexican, Indian, French, Japanese or whatever takes your fancy. In Bridgetown there are several cheap canteens for office workers where you can get a filling lunch for around US$6, and around the island there are beach bars for lunch, especially seafood and barbecue grills, and you can make a day of it with cocktails and sun loungers on the sand. But what is lacking are Bajan restaurants serving cheap, local food in the evenings. Apart from a few rum shops selling fried chicken and some fast-food places, there's not much at the budget end of the scale after dark. However, on a Friday night, **Oistins Fish Fry** is a major event for both Barbadians and tourists; see box, page 76. VAT is usually included in menu prices but a service charge of 10% is added to the bill; most menus stipulate what is and what is not included.

Bridgetown

The capital of Barbados, Bridgetown, sits on Carlisle Bay on the southwest corner of the island and has a population of around 110,000. The centre is small and compact but always busy and full of life. Swan Street is a lively pedestrian street where Barbadians do their shopping and street musicians sometimes perform; on Broad Street you will find a whole range of sophisticated shops catering for tourists, with shopping malls, duty-free shops and department stores. On the northern side of the Careenage is National Heroes Square, which celebrates the 10 figures that shaped the modern history of Barbados, and the pleasant wooden Bridgetown Boardwalk, where old converted warehouses and restaurants overlook boats plying their trade on the inlet. Another interesting place to visit is the Garrison Historic Area; inscribed as a UNESCO World Heritage Site in 2011, it has a horse-racing track and a number of fine old buildings dating back to the British colonial times. The suburbs of Bridgetown sprawl along the south and west coasts, and quite a long way inland; many areas are very pleasant, full of flowering trees and 19th-century coral stone gingerbread villas.

Broad Street and around

Previously called Cheapside, Exchange Street and New England Street, Broad Street is Bridgetown's main road and business area and is lined with shops, small malls, banks, offices and fast-food restaurants. It runs east to west from Fairchild Street to Cheapside Road, and colonial-style buildings dating back to the 1800s rub shoulders with more modern buildings. Many of the shops are devoted to cruise ship passengers and sell souvenirs and duty-free jewellery, cameras, cosmetics, alcoholic beverages and the like. The most notable is the **Cave Shepherd Department Store** ① *10-14 Broad St, T629 4400, www.mycaveshepherd.com, Mon-Thu 0830-1730, Fri 0830-1830, Sat 0830-1600*, near the top end of Broad Street close to National Heroes Square. Now a large duty-free shop, this was established by Bridgetown businessmen, Mr R G Cave and Mr J P Shepherd as a dry goods store in 1907. At the lower end of Broad Street, on the corner of Prince Alfred Street, look out for the beautiful **Mutual Building**, which was built in 1895 as the Barbados Mutual Life Assurance Society Building and is presently a branch of First Citizens Bank. It is a very tall, grey Victorian structure topped with twin silver domes and a fine overhanging iron veranda on the second floor. In 2011 it became a designated property within the UNESCO World Heritage Site of Historic Bridgetown and its Garrison.

East towards the Deep Water Harbour and next to the **General Post Office**, **Cheapside Public Market** ① *Cheapside Rd, T426 4463, Mon-Sat 0700-1700*, is an excellent

Tip...
The best time to visit Cheapside Public Market is on a Saturday morning, when many Bridgetown people shop for their weekly fresh produce and it is a hive of activity and colourful characters.

Essential Bridgetown

Finding your feet

The Adams Barrow Cummins (ABC) Highway runs from the Grantley Adams International Airport in Christ Church in the east, to Cave Hill Road and the University of the West Indies in Saint Michael on the west coast, and roughly skirts the metropolitan area of Bridgetown. Several roundabouts along the highway give access into Bridgetown. There is also a road along the south coast, Highway 7, which runs from Oistins in the east, through the main resort area on the south coast and enters the city through the Garrison Historical Area. Highway 1 runs down the west coast which comes into the capital as the Spring Gardens Highway. Buses and route taxis run frequently on all these

routes in and out of Bridgetown; out-of-town bus stops are marked simply 'To City' or 'Out of City'.

Getting around

The centre of Bridgetown is easily toured on foot, while buses, route taxis and taxis are available for venturing further afield.

Tip...
On the JTC Ramsay roundabout at the junction of the ABC Highway and Highway 5, keep an eye out for the striking, bronze, 2.75-m-high Bussa Emancipation Statue, which is of slave rebellion leader Bussa "breaking from chains".

and colourful fresh fruit and vegetable market in both a double-storey indoor part and an outdoor section of stalls. There's a great assortment of Caribbean produce for sale, like sweet potatoes, yams, eddos, breadfruits, green bananas and cassavas, and some stalls sell souvenirs such as bags, hats, sundresses and T-shirts. Upstairs there are food stalls; look out for saltfish bake, fried plantain and breadfruit and ginger and cucumber iced drinks.

National Heroes Square

This small, triangular 'square', between Broad Street and the north side of the Careenage, is the hub of central Bridgetown. It used to be called Trafalgar Square and there is a statue there of Lord Nelson, sculpted by Sir Richard Westmacott and predating its London equivalent by 30 years. Admiral Nelson visited Barbados with his fleet in 1805, a few months before his death, and the square was named the following year; the statue was erected on 22 March 1813 to commemorate the anniversary of the British Royal Navy's victory in the Battle of Trafalgar in 1805. Over the years the name became the subject of some controversy as it was thought to link Barbados too closely with its colonial past. As a result, Nelson was turned through 180° so that he no longer looked down Broad Street, and in 1999 Trafalgar Square was renamed National Heroes Square after the 10 people who

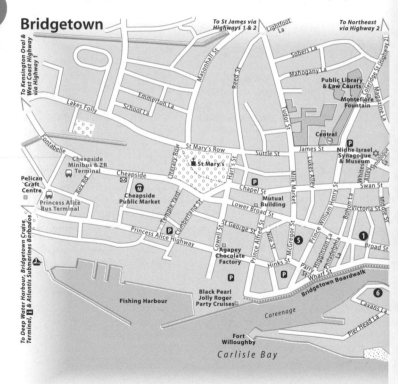

Bridgetown

shaped the modern history of Barbados; they are also remembered on National Heroes Day, which was first celebrated on 28 April 1998, the centenary of the birth of Sir Grantley Adams. Other features of the square are the Cenotaph War Memorial, with its grey granite obelisk built in 1925 to commemorate Barbadians who died during the First World War, and the Dolphin Fountain, constructed in 1865 to commemorate the piping of water to Bridgetown in 1861.

Parliament Buildings

Across Broad Street to the north of the square are the neo-Gothic Parliament Buildings with their red roofs and green shutters. Founded in 1639, Barbados has the third-oldest parliament in the Commonwealth, after Britain and Bermuda. The present buildings, where both the lower house (House of Assembly) and the upper house (Senate) still meet weekly, were completed in 1873. The east wing, housing the House of Assembly and Senate, has stained-glass windows depicting British kings and queens from James I to Queen Victoria, as well as the Lord Protector Oliver Cromwell. The **clock tower** on the west wing dates from 1886 and was originally located on the east wing; but within 10 years of its construction, it began to sink and crack and had to be demolished in 1884. The redesigned clock tower

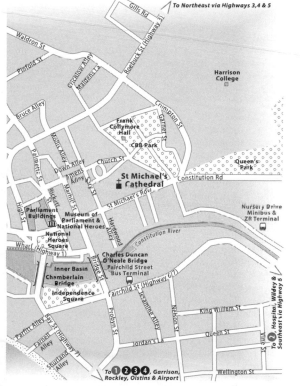

Where to stay 🛏
Nautilus Beach
 Apartments **1**
Sweetfield Manor **2**

Restaurants 🍴
Balcony **1**
Brown Sugar **2**
Cuz's Fish Stand **3**
Lobster Alive **4**
Mustors Harbour **5**
Waterfront Café **6**

BACKGROUND

Bridgetown

Bridgetown was once known as Indian Bridge, named after a basic wooden bridge across the Careenage. It is believed that the bridge was left behind by the Arawak Indians or Caribs who had inhabited the island before the 1500s. The British removed the structure and built a new bridge sometime after 1654 and the area became known as the Town of Saint Michael and, later, Bridgetown. The Careenage is an inlet of water at the mouth of Constitution River, where schooners and trading vessels transporting sugar, rum and molasses to the larger ships in Carlisle Bay used to tie up. It got its name because the boats were careened onto their sides so that the hulls could be cleaned or mended. In 1657, a portion of the waterfront was declared a public wharf; between 1837 and 1846 a new extended wharf was constructed under the direction of the Royal Engineers stationed with the British Garrison; and in 1889 the Bridgetown Dry Dock was added. By the end of the 1800s Bridgetown was a major centre for ship maintenance and repair in the Caribbean; the island was often the first landfall for ships coming from Europe. Nowadays, cargo and cruise ships dock at the Deep Water Harbour to the north, which is still one of the most advanced ports in the Caribbean; it has been dredged so it can accommodate the largest cruise ships in the world. But the Careenage is still used for recreational and tourist-based small craft such as catamarans and sport fishing boats that tout their wares to visitors. Two bridges now separate the outer and inner basins of the Careenage – Chamberlain Bridge and Charles Duncan O'Neal Bridge – and in 1999, the Wickham Lewis Boardwalk was built along Wharf Road on the northern side.

and reassembled clock were moved to the west wing in 1880. Today the west wing houses public offices as well as the **Museum of Parliament and National Heroes Gallery** ① *T310 5400, www.barbadosparliament.com, Mon, Wed-Fri 1000-1600, Sat 1000-1500, US$5, children (3-18) US$2.50*. This is a simple but well-staffed and interesting museum which brings snippets of Barbados' history alive with murals, artefacts, quotes and, for more modern events, videos and photographs. It's also refreshingly air conditioned, so makes a fine cooling break on a hot walk around the centre of Bridgetown. The National Heroes Gallery is particularly interesting, documenting the achievements of the nine men and one woman. Admission includes a guided tour of both houses of Parliament (if the Senate or the House of Assembly are sitting on the day, you can re-use your ticket on another day).

Chamberlain Bridge and around

Running south from the square is Chamberlain Bridge, for centuries one of the capital's two main bridges and built roughly in the same place as the old Indian Bridge. It was originally a swing bridge constructed between 1861 and 1872 and was named at the beginning of the 20th century in honour of Joseph Chamberlain, British Secretary of State for the Colonies, who gave the island a large chunk of money in grants and loans to keep the economy afloat. In 2005 the bridge was demolished after bits started falling off it and was rebuilt using modern materials. It reopened in 2006 as a pedestrian and lift bridge – to allow entry for boats into the inner basin of the Careenage – adjoining the refurbished coral stone arch structure dating from 1861. There is a plaque with the Barbados national anthem on the bridge, while **Independence Arch**, at the southern end of the bridge, was built in 1987 to celebrate 21 years of independence; look out for some of the national symbols painted on the pillars, including a flying fish, a pelican and the Pride of Barbados flower.

To the east of the arch and bridge and running between the southern side of the Careenage and Fairchild Street to Charles Duncan O'Neal Bridge (see below), Independence Square – formerly a car park – is a recreational square and garden with a view across the inner basin of the Careenage to National Heroes Square and Parliament Buildings. It has seating areas, an amphitheatre for public events, two fountains and a bronze statue of Errol Walton Barrow, the first Prime Minister of Barbados (1966-1976) who had a political career that lasted 36 years up until his death in 1987; he is one of the 10 National Heroes of Barbados.

To the west of Chamberlain Bridge, along Wharf Street on the northern side of the Careenage, is the wooden **Bridgetown Boardwalk**. Its official name is **Wickham Lewis Boardwalk**, after Clennell Wickham (1896-1938), a radical journalist and newspaper editor, and TT Lewis (1905-1959), a politician. Featuring vintage-style street lamps and benches and a number of shops and cafés, a stroll along here gives a good view of the yachts, charter fishing boats and catamarans docked in the Careenage. About halfway along, on the corner of Parry Street, the red-brick **Old Spirit Bond Mall** building dates back to the 18th century when it was a warehouse for rum and other spirits. From here, barrels were loaded on to small boats in the Careenage and then transported to cargo ships docked offshore in Carlisle Bay. The building has been restored as a mall with a number of small shops. At the western end of the boardwalk is a small park which celebrates Barbados' maritime heritage, complete with cannons (originally from James Fort) and plaques with interesting facts about Barbados pirates. At the Carlisle Wharf Building is the office for **Black Pearl Jolly Roger Party Cruises** ① *T826 7245, www.barbadosblackpearl-jollyroger1.com, see also page 97*, which offers cruises on a replica pirate boat. The **Agapey Chocolate Factory** ① *Hincks St, T426 8505, www.agapey.com, 1¼-hr tours Wed and Thu 0930, Fri 1100, other times available for groups, US$20 per person*, about 500 m west of Chamberlain Bridge, offers interesting 'bean to bar' tours with prior reservation; their delicious chocolate uses local cane sugar and rum to flavour cocoa from Ecuador, Grenada and the Dominican Republic.

Charles Duncan O'Neal Bridge

The second bridge over the Careenage, going off southeast from National Heroes Square, is named after another of the National Heroes of Barbados, Charles Duncan O'Neal (1879-1936), a physician by trade who worked on behalf of the poor and the disadvantaged and established the Democratic League in 1924 and the Working Men's Association in 1926; in 1932 he was elected to the House of Assembly. The first bridge here was completed in 1681 and was funded by levying a tax on slaves. It was pulled down in 1967 and replaced with a wider, stronger, more modern structure designed to take the increased volume of traffic. If you are driving, the junctions can be a bit scary until you get the hang of the one-way system as locals drive very fast over the river and away; the Fairchild Street Bus Terminal creates an extra hazard on the south side of the bridge.

St Michael's Cathedral

St Michael's Row, T427 0790, see Facebook. Mon-Fri 0730-1700, Sat 0900-1300, Sun services between 0715 and 1800, free but donations appreciated.

Take the northeast exit out of National Heroes Square along St Michael's Row to reach the 18th-century Anglican St Michael's Cathedral (also known as **All Angels**). It has a fine set of inscriptions and a single-hand clock. The first building was consecrated in 1665 but destroyed by a hurricane in 1780. The present cathedral is long and broad with a balcony. It has a huge barrel-vaulted ceiling, at one time the widest in the world, galleries on three sides, stained-glass windows and some tombs (1675) built into the porch. Completed in 1789 with £10,000 raised in a lottery, it became a cathedral in 1825 with the arrival of Bishop Coleridge, but suffered hurricane damage in 1831. Sir Grantley Adams and his son, Tom Adams, both prime ministers, are buried here along with other famous Barbadians.

Queen's Park and around

If you continue east on St Michael's Row, you reach Queen's Park, a pleasant, restful park just outside the city centre, which shares parts of its grounds with Harrison College and the headquarters of the Barbados Transport Board. It's home to the largest tree in Barbados: a 28-m-tall baobab with a circumference of 18 m, thought to be over 1000 years old. Baobabs originated in Guinea and the tree is believed to have floated across the Atlantic and rooted itself on the edge of a lagoon. The park and its fountain were designed by Lady Gilbert Carter, the wife of the governor, who opened the gates in 1909 with a golden key. **Queen's Park House**, a beautiful building dating from 1786, was once the residence of the general commanding the British troops in the West Indies (it was known as King's House until Queen Victoria came to the throne); in the 20th century it became a small theatre (Daphne Joseph-Hackett Theatre) and art gallery. However, the house is now boarded up and the Queen's Park Gallery is located in the Pelican Craft Centre on Princess Alice Highway (see page 93).

Further east still is **Government House**, first known as Pilgrim House. It was purchased for the Government in 1736 from John Pilgrim, a Quaker. It is a typical example of a plantation great house, with arched porticoes, jalousie window shutters, verandas, a parapet roof and a circular driveway, as well as delightful gardens. The home and office of the Governor General of Barbados, it is sometimes included in the Barbados National Trust's Open House Programme (see box, page 18).

Swan Street

Back in the centre and parallel to Broad Street, busy Swan Street is the second most popular shopping area in Bridgetown. It was named after John Swann, the surveyor who laid out the principal streets in 1656. In the early years it was also known as Jew Street because it was mainly populated by Jewish merchants, who had shops and businesses on the ground level and lived upstairs; by the late 17th century, Jews had almost exclusive control over imported goods from Europe. After a destructive fire in 1845, this street, along with many properties in the lower Bridgetown area, became known as the 'Burnt District'. Today Swan Street is a pedestrian cobblestone street lined with shops and stalls (generally cheaper than on Broad Street).

Nidhe Israel Synagogue and Museum

Synagogue Lane, T436 6869, see Facebook. Mon-Fri 0900-1600, weekends by appointment only, US$12.50, children (5-12) US$6, under 5s free.

A block north of Swan Street, this beautifully restored place of worship is an early 19th-century building on the site of a 17th-century one, one of the two earliest synagogues in the western hemisphere. The original one was built in 1654 by Jews fleeing Recife, Brazil, who heard that Oliver Cromwell had granted freedom of worship for Jews. Cromwell granted the first pass to settle in 1655 to Dr Abraham de Mercado, an elder of the Recife society, and his son David Rafael. By the 1680s there were 300 Jews in Barbados, or 5% of the total population, and by the middle of the 18th century there were 800. They were heavily involved in the sugar industry, advancing capital and credit or owning plantations; their influence was so great that Swan Street was once known as Jew Street. The synagogue was destroyed by a hurricane in 1831, and the present building was constructed on the old foundations and re-opened in 1833. But by 1929 the Jewish community on the island had all but migrated and the synagogue fell into disrepair.

A small revival of Jewish residents on the island began with a few Polish Jews fleeing Europe in the late 1930s en route to Venezuela. They started working as peddlers and gradually attracted friends and other family members and the community grew again. Painstakingly restored by this community, with the support of the Barbados National Trust, the Caribbean Conservation Association and the Barbados government, the synagogue reopened in 2008. In 2011 it became a designated property within the UNESCO World Heritage Site of Historic Bridgetown and its Garrison. The museum is in the former rabbi's house next to the synagogue; exhibits include a timeline of Jewish settlement in Barbados. In the grounds is a full immersion *mikvah*, which dates back to the 17th century and is the only one known to exist in the Americas.

Coleridge Street

Near the synagogue, in a block along Coleridge Street, are the **Public Library**, founded by Andrew Carnegie, the **Law Courts** and the **Central Police Station**. At one time the Legislature, the Law Courts and the Jail were on this site, leading Henry Nelson Coleridge to write in 1832: "His Majesty's Council, the General Assembly, the Judge, the juries, the debtors and the felons, all live together in the same house". In a small garden on the other side of the road opposite the library, is the **Montefiore Fountain**. It was built as a drinking water fountain in 1864 by John Montefiore in memory of his father, a leading merchant who died of cholera. It was originally in Beckwith Place, Lower Broad Street but was moved to Coleridge Street in 1940 and there is no water connected to it. The statues on each face of the fountain represent Justice, Fortitude, Temperance and Prudence.

Bay Street

Bay Street runs south of the city centre from the two bridges and Independence Square, hugging the edge of **Carlisle Bay**, which was named after the Earl of Carlisle, James Hay, who was Lord Proprietor of Barbados in the 1600s. Bay Street is part of Highway 7, the main route between Bridgetown and the south coast. Along this part of the bay is **Brownes Beach**, which has broad white sands, calm, clear water with small waves and almost no undertow. It is a surprisingly good beach considering how close it is to town. Yachts anchor here, snorkelling and diving parties call in and there are beach facilities such as sun loungers and umbrellas and lifeguards are on duty. With beach bars and restaurants and a number of watersports operators, it's a lively area with lots of action and is often packed with cruise ship visitors.

At the northern end of Brownes Beach, **The Boatyard** ⓘ *Bay St, T826 4448, www. theboatyard.com, daily 0900-2000, restaurant 1100-1700, day pass US$25, children (under 6) US$12.50; other packages include food and drinks*, is a beach club with sun loungers and umbrellas, a waterslide, an ocean trampoline, a floating 'mountain climbing iceberg', changing facilities, lockers, showers and toilets, non-stop music, and a bar and restaurant. Jet skis, banana-boat rides and glass-bottom boat tours can be organized. On Friday evenings the restaurant hours extend to 2200 for a Fish Fry event when no entry fee is required if you're eating.

At the southern end of the beach, opposite the Prime Minister's Office, is the Bay Street Esplanade – a small park and promenade featuring a bandstand dating from 1919 and a statue of Sir Grantley Adams. It has benches and lawns popular for barbecues and sunset-watching. A little further south on Pebbles Beach and accessed from Bay Street are the island's two sailing clubs. The **Barbados Yacht Club** ⓘ *T427 1125, www.barbadosyachtclub.com*, is a private members' club (visiting yachts are given a seven-day membership) that holds colourful regattas in Carlisle Bay at weekends throughout the year. The largest is the **Mount Gay Rum Barbados Regatta**, usually in the middle of May. The **Barbados Cruising Club** ⓘ *T426 4434, www.barbadoscruisingclub.org*, is again a private members' club that hosts Barbados' biggest sailing event each year: the **Mount Gay Round Barbados Race** and the **Ocean Passage Race to Antigua** (www.mountgayrumroundbarbadosrace.com), which attracts hundreds of racing boats from all over the Caribbean and is sailed over three days, usually in the middle of January. This is a wonderful event to watch from Bay Street and the races can also be seen from various points around the island.

The offshore **Carlisle Bay Marine Park** is a favourite spot for diving and snorkelling excursions, with a series of interlocking marine trails roughly marked out underwater by old cannons, anchors and pylons leading the way from one wreck to the next. There are five shallow wrecks in the bay: the *Berwyn*, the *Fox*, the *C-Trec*, the *Bajan Queen* and the *Eillon*. The *Bajan Queen*, a tugboat converted to a party boat before being sunk in 2002, sits only a few metres underwater so is perfect for snorkelling or diving, and is growing a variety of coral as well as being home to plenty of fish. The *Berwyn* was a French First World War tugboat sunk in 1919 by her own crew; because of her age, this wreck is covered in healthy hard and soft coral growth and associated reef creatures.

★Garrison Historic Area
an excellent example of 18th-century British military architecture

South of central Bridgetown is the Garrison area on the strategic southeast point of the island guarding the entrance to Carlisle Bay and the capital. During the 18th century the Caribbean was the scene of numerous military conflicts, primarily between Britain and France who fought for supremacy. In the face of a possible French invasion in 1785, a permanent garrison was built and Barbados became the headquarters of the Windward and Leeward command of the British forces in the region. It was the largest of its kind in the British Colonies, and included hospitals, barracks and houses in the Georgian and Palladian style with grand staircases, arcades and pediments. But by the late 19th century the British decided to reduce their forces in the region, and by 1905 most of the last regiments had left the island. In 2011, Historic Bridgetown and its Garrison became a UNESCO World Heritage Site as "an outstanding example of British colonial architecture" and today there are a number of historically significant buildings to visit.

Garrison Savannah
The 61-ha (151-acre) Garrison Historic Area covers an area from the Bay Street Esplanade to Hastings on the south coast. The focal point is the 13-ha (30-acre) Garrison Savannah (or just the 'Savannah'), once a swamp before it was drained by the Royal Engineers in the early 1800s to become a parade ground for soldiers and the place where they trained and drilled. It was surrounded by a six-furlong racecourse in 1845, first used by regimental officers whose horses competed against those of wealthy plantation owners. Still a popular racecourse, it is now the home of the **Barbados Turf Club** (see box, opposite), and is used

ON THE ROAD
Horsing around

Horse racing is surprisingly popular on the Caribbean islands, where there is sufficient flat land to build a race track and even on some where there isn't. Like many sports it is seen as an opportunity for a party and the crowd is enthusiastic, even if not particularly knowledgeable, although never underestimate the locals when it comes to betting. In Bridgetown there has been horse racing on the Garrison Savannah since 1845 and the **Barbados Turf Club** (T626 3980, www.barbadosturfclub.org, ticket office at the Grandstand, Monday-Friday 0800-1600) was established in 1905. The track is a 6-furlong oval grass strip with the horses running in a clockwise direction. The Grandstand gives you a good vantage point becuse it is elevated, but anywhere around the track is good to watch the racing, and you can get right up close to the action by the parade ring, the finish line or when the jockeys make their way to the weighing room. The betting booths and food and drink stalls are never far away and there is entertainment from 1300-1800.

The most prestigious event of the year is the Sandy Lane Barbados Gold Cup, a thoroughbred race run annually in late February/early March since 1982 and sponsored by Sandy Lane since 1997. The Gold Cup attracts racehorse owners from around the world. There are crowds, stalls, noise, merriment and lots of entertainment from dancers to regimental bands. Nine races are held on the day with the most important being the penultimate one that is run over a distance of 1800 m (8.95 furlongs). All the excitement builds up to see who will win the gold trophy, usually presented to the winner by the Prime Minister of Barbados. At other times of the year, race meetings are held on Saturday afternoons during three seasons: January-April, May-August and October-December. Entry to the Grandstand is US$10, children (under 12) US$5, and to the Field Stand and Sir John Chandler Stand, the flatter areas on either side of the Grandstand and around the track, US$5, children (under 12) free. Higher entry fees apply for the Sandy Lane Barbados Gold Cup and Boxing Day races.

at other times for exercising the horses, early morning or evening jogging, informal rugby and basketball games and there's usually something going on on Sunday afternoons. Along Garrison Road and the roads leading off are numerous 17th- to 19th-century military buildings constructed on traditional British colonial lines from brick brought as ballast on ships from England. Painted in bright colours, some now contain government offices, others are places of business or private homes. There are several memorials around the oval racecourse. In the southwest corner is one commemorating the 'awful' hurricane which killed 14 men and one woman and caused the destruction of the barracks and hospital on 18 August 1831; outside the Barbados Museum in the northeast corner there's another to the men of the Royal York Rangers who fell in action against the French in Martinique, Les Saintes and Guadeloupe in the 1809-1810 campaign.

Tip...
Each site in the Garrison Historic Area can be visited independently, but the Barbados Garrison Historical Consortium also offers guided tours; visit the website (www.barbadosgarrison.net) or Facebook page for more information.

Main Guard

On Garrison Road, the Main Guard overlooks the racecourse from the western side. Built in 1804, it is one of the most outstanding buildings in the Garrison Historic Area. It is of elegant Georgian style and the main house, with its Roman arched portico and pediment, has a George III Coat of Arms designed especially for the building, a handsome clock tower, a fine wide veranda (or gallery in Caribbean terms) with cast-iron trimmings, and there's a guardhouse at the rear. It was used as the main guard command and central military police station during the 1800s until 1905 when the British forces withdrew. Today the property is home to several organizations, including the Barbados Garrison Historical Consortium, Barbados Legion and Barbados Poppy League. Outside is an impressive array of 26 cannons (part of the National Cannon Collection, see page 42) mounted on metal garrison gun carriages (replaced with wooden ones during action as they were prone to shatter).

Tip...

Every Thursday, the Barbados Legion pays tribute to the military history of Barbados by re-enacting the Changing of the Sentry ceremony at the Main Guard. Up to 13 men in full ceremonial dress – the Zouave uniform selected by Queen Victoria in 1858 for the West India Regiment – march past the sentry post at the clock tower. This presentation starts at 1145 and lasts approximately 15 minutes until the clock chimes at noon (the sentries take their annual holiday in September).

Barbados Museum

Dalkeith Rd, T427 0201, www.barbmuse.org.bb. Mon-Sat 0900-1700, Sun 1400-1800, US$10, children (under 12) US$5.

On the northeast corner of the Savannah, this museum is housed in the former British Military Prison; its upper section was built in 1817 and lower section in 1853. It became the Barbados Museum and headquarters of the Historical Society from 1930. It is well set out through a series of 10 galleries, and exhibits include a fine map gallery with the earliest map of Barbados by Richard Ligon (1657), colonial furniture, military history (including a reconstruction of a prisoner's cell), prints and paintings which depict social life in the West Indies, decorative and domestic arts (17th- to 19th-century glass, china and silver), and a gallery about slavery and African people in the Caribbean. The staff are very knowledgeable about the history of the island and the museum shop has a good selection of craft items, books, prints and cards.

George Washington House and Garrison Tunnels

Bush Hill, off Garrison Rd, T228 5461, see Facebook. Mon-Fri 0900-1630, US$10, children (5-12) US$5, under 5s free; Garrison Tunnels, 15-min tours available Mon-Fri 0900-1600, US$10/5, combination ticket for house and tunnels, US$15/US$7.50.

North of the Main Guard at the northwest corner of the Savannah, this beautifully restored 18th-century plantation house is where the future first president of the USA stayed in 1751 for a few months when, as a 19 year old, he accompanied his sick brother Lawrence (who later died) to search for a cure for his TB. This was George Washington's only excursion outside his homeland and Bridgetown was the largest town he had seen. At that time, health care was more advanced in Barbados than it was in the United States. While in Bridgetown, Washington was introduced to the delights of the theatre and banquets

Beards and Bims – the naming of Barbados

A number of theories exist as to how the island got its name(s). Portuguese explorer Pedro a Campos 'discovered' Barbados in 1536 en route to Brazil, and it was he who named the island Los Barbados, which means 'the bearded ones'. It is unclear whether 'bearded' refers to the long, hanging roots of the bearded fig-tree (*Ficus citrifolia*), indigenous to the island, or to the allegedly heavily bearded Caribs who once inhabited the island; or perhaps it was a visual impression of a beard of white foam created by breaking waves over the outlying reefs that would have been seen by the early sailors. Other names or nicknames associated with Barbados are 'Bim' and 'Bimshire', and again several theories exist. Bim could have been a corruption of the surname Byam, after Lieutenant General William Byam, a Royalist leader faithful to the crown during the Civil War. Soon after the war began (1642) Byam was imprisoned in the Tower of London, but later accepted a pass to be exiled to Barbados. After the war, many other Royalists fled to the Caribbean and, following the execution of Charles I (1649), Barbados' government fell under the control of these Royalists. In 1651, parliament in England decided they would need to take back the island again and, after some skirmishing, the Royalists were defeated by the British Navy. This time Byam was banished from Barbados and went to Suriname in South America. It is said that his followers became known as 'Bims' and that this became a name for all Barbadians. A second theory is that 'Bim' is derived from a word meaning 'my home', 'my people' or 'those that lived there' in the language of the Igbo people of West Africa, many of whom arrived from modern-day southeastern Nigeria as slaves in the 18th century. Over time, and long before the island's independence, Barbados became known as 'Bimshire', an affectionate reference to its long colonial relationship with England.

where he met the leading scientists, engineers and military strategists of the day. He contracted smallpox but the skill of a British doctor saved him. As a result, he acquired immunity to the virus which enabled him to survive an outbreak of the disease during the American War of Independence, which killed many of his men.

The house went on to become Bush Hill House, a residence for officers within the Garrison, including the Commander of the Royal Engineers. After the withdrawal of the British in 1905, it returned to private ownership until it was restored and opened to the public in 2007. The ground floor is furnished as it might have been in 1751 when Washington stayed, while the second floor displays items typical of life in the mid-18th century, from medical appliances to agricultural implements; there's a section on the plantation economy and slavery and how it related to Washington, a slave owner himself.

Access to the Garrison Tunnels is from George Washington House. The tunnel below the house was re-discovered

Tip...
Coffee Barbados Café, in the old 1830s stable building of George Washington House (T271 0376, Monday-Friday 0730-1600, Saturday 0900-1600) serves breakfast, lunch and cakes/pastries and has a wonderful view of the gardens (you can visit without paying house entry fees).

quite by accident in 2011 during preparation work for the relocation of the café. After exploration, this tunnel was found to extend far beyond the boundaries of the property and joins a 3-km network of at least nine other tunnels under the Savannah area, with others extending into the west of the Garrison's 61 ha (151 acres). The restored section under George Washington House that is open to the public is about 60 m in length, 60 cm wide and 2.5-3.5 m high. It is believed that these mysterious arched-roof tunnels carved through limestone rock date from about 1820 and were used as a drainage course for the then swampy Savannah, and also to facilitate the secret movement of soldiers.

St Anne's Fort

South of the Main Guard on the southwest side of the Savannah, St Anne's Fort was built in 1705 and, during the 1800s, a lookout was added and it became the main command post and communication point for the six signal stations located around the island. The long, thin Drill Hall was built on to the walls of the fort in 1790 as barracks for the soldiers, and in 1881 the building became the headquarters for the Garrison until the British left in 1905. In 1979, it became the Officers' Mess and Sergeants' Mess of the Barbados Defence Force, and the fort remains their headquarters today. You cannot enter but look for the crenellated signal tower with its flagpole on top.

The **Barbados National Armoury** ① *access via the Barbados Defence Force reception, T427 1436, or enquire at the office at the Main Guard, 1½-hr tours by appointment only, Mon-Fri 1000, US\$25 for 1-5 people, US\$5 per additional person up to 12*, is in the old naval powder magazine of St Anne's Fort. It displays the majority of the **Barbados National Cannon Collection** (also known as the National Ordnance Collection of Barbados) and, with more than 400 great guns, is considered the world's rarest collection of 17th- and 18th-century English iron cannons. Some have royal seals from Charles II, Queen Anne, the King Georges and Queen Victoria. The most famous is the 1650 Commonwealth Gun, which bears the Coat of Arms of Oliver Cromwell; only one of two in the world (the other is in the Tower of London). A further 26 cannons from the National Cannon Collection can be seen in front of the Main Guard and Clock Tower looking on to the Garrison Savannah (see page 40). The armoury also exhibits military memorabilia such as copies of old maps and colourful portraits of soldiers, and the tour includes a quick glimpse of the still-used 19th-century barracks. The late Mike Hartland, a major in the Barbados Defence Force, was the driving force behind the gathering of this unique collection, which was established in 2002. He found many of the guns from all along the west and south coasts of Barbados in gardens, cellars, on beaches, embedded in the sides of buildings and buried under fortifications.

Charles Fort and around

To the west of St Anne's Fort, off Drill Hall Beach Road, and in the gardens of the Hilton Barbados Resort at Needhams Point, Charles Fort was built in 1650 and was the largest of the many forts which guarded the south and west coasts. Originally called Needhams Fort, the name was changed in 1660 when King Charles II regained the throne after Charles I was beheaded. In 1836 the fort was incorporated into the Garrison. Today, only the ramparts remain but there are a number of 24-pounder cannons dating from 1824 pointing out to sea, and there a good view across Carlisle Bay. Also in the Hilton's grounds, the **Military Cemetery** dates back to 1780; the headstones make interesting reading – it appears, for instance, that disease claimed more lives than military action. Visible only from the beach to the south of the Hilton, the disused **Needhams Point Lighthouse**, octagonal in shape, was built in 1855. When it was in use, it had a half-red, half-green stationary light that let approaching vessels know if they were port or starboard of Carlisle Bay.

Harry Bayley Observatory

Observatory Rd, Clapham, St Michael (about 4.5 km west of central Bridgetown), T622 2000, www.hbo.bb. Fri 2000-2200, US$10, children (5-12) US$5, under 5s free. To get there take Highway 7 and then turn off on to Beckles Rd and then Brittons Cross Rd and the observatory is on the left.

In the Clapham residential area and named after Dr Harry Bayley, a keen amateur astronomer who founded the Barbados Astronomical Society, the observatory is open to the public once a week (weather permitting). Built in 1963 (and refurbished in 2014), it is the only observatory in the Eastern Caribbean and is a chance for northern visitors to look through a 16-inch reflector telescope at the southern hemisphere stars and planets, which aren't all visible from North America and Europe. The moon, Jupiter and Saturn can all be seen on a cloudless night.

Tyrol Cot Heritage Village

Codrington Hill, St Michael (about 4 km north of central Bridgetown), T424 2074, www. barbadosnationaltrust.org. Mon-Fri 0800-1600, free. To get there, the most direct route is via Whitepark Rd and Lower Bank Hall Main Rd and then turn left on to Codrington Rd past the National Stadium.

Built in 1854 by William Farnum, this attraction is preserved for posterity by the Barbados National Trust for being the home, from 1929, of Sir Grantley Adams, the founder of the Barbados Labour Party, prime minister of the short-lived West Indies Federation and of the newly independent Barbados. It was also the birthplace of his son, Tom Adams, who was prime minister from 1976 to 1985. After the death of Sir Grantley Adams' wife Grace (in 1990), the site was opened to the public as the Tyrol Cot Heritage Village in 1995. The house is built of coral stone and ballast bricks and is furnished with all of the family's original possessions dating from the 1930s, complete with mahogany furniture, books, antique glass and ceramics, and other memorabilia. The Chattel House Village on the 1.6 ha (4 acres) of grounds is a replica of how a 1920s Barbadian village would have looked, with a barber's shop, blacksmith's forge and rum shop. However, it's presently not in great shape – the interiors are gloomy and dusty, the artisan's craft shops haven't been operational for some years and it is poorly staffed. It is sometimes included in the Barbados National Trust's Open House Programme (see box, page 18) when guides and talks make a visit more interesting.

St George Parish Church

Highway 4B, The Glebe, St George, about 8.5 km northeast of central Bridgetown, T436 8794, www.anglican.bb. Open daily 0600-1800, free but donations appreciated.

After the original church dating from 1637 was destroyed in the hurricane of 1780, another, built on the same site four years later, survived the next great hurricane of 1831, and remained intact during those of 1898 and 1955, making it the oldest ecclesiastical building on the island. Inside there is a magnificent altar painting of the Resurrection by Benjamin West, the first American president of the Royal Academy, a post he held from 1792 until his death in 1820. King George III was a patron of Benjamin West and many of his paintings hang in Buckingham Palace. There are also marble sculptures by Richard Westmacott, the creator of the statue of Lord Nelson in National Heroes Square, Bridgetown.

Gun Hill Signal Station

Gun Hill, Fusilier Rd, Newbury, St George, T429 3235. Mon-Sat 0900-1700, US$5, children (under 12) US$2.50.

A five-minute drive from the St George Parish Church heading uphill, the approach to Gun Hill is by Fusilier Road where you will pass the white lion carved by British soldiers in 1868 before turning left to the Signal Station. This road was built by Royal Scot Fusiliers between September 1862 and February 1863 when they were stationed at Gun Hill to avoid contracting yellow fever. The signal station itself was initially constructed in 1816 when it was decided that a military presence would be maintained outside Bridgetown in case of slave uprisings. The strategically placed hexagonal tower was one of a chain of six signal stations across the island that were also used to communicate news and messages using flags and lantern codes. Today Gun Hill is maintained by the Barbados National Trust and houses a collection of military memorabilia, although the real reason to come here is to enjoy the incredible view. Informative guides will explain the workings of the signal station and point out interesting features of the surrounding countryside. There is a small café called **Fusiliers**.

Tip...
The view from Gun Hill is one of the most expansive on the island, taking in the whole of the south coast across to Bridgetown harbour.

Orchid World and Tropical Flower Garden

Groves, St George, T433 0306, www.orchidworldbarbados.com. Daily 0900-1600, 15 May-1 Nov closed Mon. US$10, children (5-13) US$5, under 4s free. The Sergeant St bus from Fairchild St Bus Terminal, Bridgetown, stops outside the entrance.

Located between Gun Hill and St John's Church on Highway 3B in St George, some 30,000 orchids are grown in this 2.4-ha (6-acre) garden in a beautiful, mind-blowing display; don't miss this. They come from all over the world, some being grown in full sun, trained on wire fences so their roots don't touch the ground, some grown on trees, some in the ground, some in coconut shells and some in 'houses' for partial shade under nets. A path meanders down the hillside, initially through woodland and past a waterfall, where orchids and other plants grow in their natural environment. Then you come out onto lawns where the path is directed between living fences of orchids, before you are bombarded with visual splendour in the orchid houses. There's a gazebo which offers a panoramic view of the valley and sugar cane fields, and a snack bar and gift shop selling orchids on tea towels, trays, mugs and numerous other souvenirs. There are also plants for sale.

West
coast

Known as the Platinum Coast with luxury wall-to-wall
low-rise hotels and villas along the seafront, the west is
not just for posh pensioners and well-heeled celebrities.
Good-quality cheaper accommodation can also be found
if you are prepared to walk a few minutes to the beach.
The strip starts just north of Bridgetown: Brandons
Beach, within the confines of town, comes first, and
then as you head up the west coast you will come to the
main tourist area around Holetown, Speightstown and
up to Little Good Harbour. Everything is accessed from
Highway 1, which is easily drivable – though always
busy with traffic – and well served by buses. Highway
2A runs parallel inland and goes through the sugar cane
heartland and gives access to a number of tourist sights.
Most of the west coast is lined with golden sand, even
the towns of Speightstown and Holetown have tempting
beaches which are clean and attractive. All beaches
are public, but access can be tricky where there is solid
development and some hotels and restaurants block you
out by denying access or cramming the sand with their
sun beds; look out for footpaths between hotels where
you can get down to the water. The beaches are narrow
and often eroded, but all have west-facing sunset views
and the sea is usually calmer here than elsewhere.

Brandons Beach and Brighton Beach

Just north of Bridgetown off Spring Garden Highway and about a 2-km walk from the Bridgetown Cruise Terminal is Brandons Beach, which has a car park, a changing facility with toilets and showers, and lifeguards. It is busy at weekends with local families but at other times is fairly quiet unless there's a cruise ship in port. **Weisers on the Bay** ① *T425 6450, www.weisersbeachbar.com, daily 0900-2200,* the casual beach bar and restaurant, has a good choice of cocktails and Bajan food (try the jerk chicken or flying fish sandwiches) and rents out sun loungers and umbrellas. Brighton Beach, just north of Brandons Beach, is very similar (car park, changing facilities and showers, sun loungers, umbrellas and lifeguards). At the northern end the 'Hot Pot' is a pool of warm water in the sand, created by a nearby power plant that pumps extremely hot water out to the ocean. Local people like to soak in it and it is clean and relaxing, but great care should be taken as there can be a strong undertow; don't swim close to the outlet pipe, and check conditions before jumping in.

Behind Brandons Beach is the **Mount Gay Visitor Centre** ① *Exmouth Gap, off Spring Garden Highway, St Michael, T428 8757, www.mountgayrum.com, gift shop Mon-Fri 0900-1700, Dec-Apr Sat 1000-1600,* where you can learn all about and taste Barbados' historic rum (the distilleries themselves are in the northern part of the island). Mount Gay's roots can be traced back to the first production of sugar cane on the island, and the oldest surviving deed for the company is from 1703, making **Mount Gay Rum** the oldest rum and continually produced spirit in the world. Today several varieties are produced including **1703, Silver, Black Barrel, Extra Old,** and the flagship **Mount Gay Eclipse.** There are four tours to choose from: the 45-minute **Signature Tasting Tour** does not require pre-booking and includes an introduction and tastings (tours depart hourly, Monday-Friday 0930-1430, December-April Saturday 1000-1430, US$15). You need to book ahead for the **Cocktail Tour** (US$65), **Barbadian Lunch Tour** (US$70) and **Rum Pairing Tour** (US$70).

Batts Rock and Paradise Beach

About 1 km north of the roundabout where Highway 1 begins, turn sharp left. Drive down to **Batts Rock Beach** and walk south to get to **Paradise Beach** via a concrete path through a shady wooded area. Batts Rock has a car park, children's playground, picnic tables, showers and changing facilities. There is a lifeguard station at Batts Rock but none at Paradise Beach. Work on a new **Four Seasons** hotel and luxury villa development at Paradise Beach is stalled, leaving an unfinished building site, and there are no signs that its financial problems will end soon. Meanwhile, the beach itself is beautiful, with calm water and many cruise ship visitors come here for the day. Swimming and snorkelling is good at both Batts Rock and Paradise Beach and there are often turtles to accompany you.

Paynes Bay

The heart of the Platinum Coast, Paynes Bay is a wide sweep of pale golden sand with trees at one end and crystal-clear water for swimming. It's a 20-minute stroll from end to end, and the northern half, away from the hotels, is usually uncrowded. There are shower and changing facilities, sun lounger and umbrella rentals, lifeguards and plenty

Tip...

There are several points of access through the resorts to the beach at Paynes Bay but parking is limited. Try the roadside just south of Sandy Lane where the trees give shade and a path leads down to the beach; otherwise park a bit further south. Plenty of buses stop on Highway 1.

ON THE ROAD
Turtles

Barbados attracts a large number of hawksbill turtles, and smaller numbers of leatherback and green turtles. Adult females return to the beaches that they themselves hatched on in order to make their own nests and lay their eggs. The hawksbill and green nest between May and October, mainly on the west and south coasts of the island, whilst the leatherback, the largest of all turtle species, nests between February and July on the windswept beaches of the east and southeast coasts. Hawksbills can often be spotted playing and feeding along the inshore reefs, at snorkelling spots on the south and west coasts, and during the nesting season visitors to these coasts have a good chance of seeing at least one nesting hawksbill during a two-week stay. A very popular activity, particularly with children, is to go on a boat trip and swim with them as they feed amongst the coral. A long history of hunting these animals for their meat, eggs and shells, has massively reduced Caribbean populations. However, turtle hunting and the possession of turtle products is illegal on Barbados and the **Barbados Sea Turtle Project** (www.barbadosseaturtles.org) has carefully monitored turtle activity for more than 25 years. During season, staff patrol high-density nesting beaches at night; when necessary they relocate nests that are too close to the high tide line, and rescue hatchlings disoriented by hotel lights or turtles that have been accidentally hooked or partially drowned in fishing nets. The project provides a 24-hour year-round **Sea Turtle Hotline** (T230 0142), which the public and visitors can use to call in information on nesting turtles, hatching of eggs, exposed eggs in the sand, or lost or injured turtles. Additionally, you can call the hotline if you are interested in witnessing the release of hatchlings, or watching the teams tagging the females, or if you want to make a donation (the project relies heavily on sponsorship).

of restaurants and beach bars in this area. Watersports are available from several outlets on the beach and activities include jet skis, kayaks, boogie boards, inflatable doughnuts, banana-boat rides and catamaran cruises. Everything is very casual and relaxed, although expect a little harassment by beach vendors. Snorkelling is good here as the little reef directly in front of Treasure Beach Hotel has colourful marine life and is quite close to the shore and there are many buoyed off areas. The green and hawksbill turtles are usually further out, roughly 250-m offshore; you need to be a strong swimmer and it is open water with jet skis and speed boats zooming by. It is better to go out on a glass-bottomed boat then you can swim around the boat with snorkelling gear. The going rate is around US$25 per person for about an hour. The best time to visit the turtles is early in the morning when they often approach and are quite curious; from around 1000, large catamarans arrive, and there can be hundreds of people in the sea.

About 2 km inland from Paynes Bay Beach on Holders Hill, is the **Barbados Polo Club** (see page 97) and on the same property is the beautiful **Holders House**, which overlooks the Old Nine golf course at Sandy Lane. A traditional Bajan plantation house dating from the 17th century with an elegant, wraparound veranda and set in 2 ha (5 acres) of formal park-like gardens with a long meandering driveway, it is available as a house rental (seven bedrooms and a state-of-the-art music studio). It also hosts the **Holders Farmers**

Sandy Lane

Backing on to the arc of golden sand at Sandy Lane Bay between Paynes Bay and Holetown, **Sandy Lane** (T444 2000, www.sandylane.com) is an institution in Barbados. You can't miss it as you drive up Highway 1, passing its grand entrance through the gracious avenue of ancient trees on the sea side of the road and the golf course on the inland side. It first opened in 1961 after Ronald Tree, a former British politician, had an idea to build a luxury hotel and golf course on what was an old sugar plantation named 'Sandy Lane' (his own beach house, **Heron Bay**, could no longer accommodate all the rich and famous people who wanted to stay there). With just 52 rooms, it quickly became known as the most elegant and sophisticated hotel in Barbados, indeed, at that time, in the Caribbean. As such it attracted a wealthy clientele that included film stars, politicians, royalty and dignitaries, all fleeing winter in the northern hemisphere for a spot of pampering in the tropical sunshine. There was a change of ownership in 1996 after which the hotel was closed for several years. It reopened in 2001, having been rebuilt, rather than refurbished. The hotel's new owners had just one goal in mind; to recreate the most distinguished address in the Caribbean but to elevate the hotel to a whole new level in line with modern expectations in the super-luxury resort market. Today it's the sort of place where butlers unpack for you and beach attendants polish your sunglasses and make sure there isn't a grain of sand on your towel. No expense is spared: everything – from an underwater sound system in the vast swimming pool, to golf carts kitted out with GPS – is designed with luxury in mind. The atmosphere is plush and, while the place is packed with celebrities in the peak winter months, it's full of normal people (albeit very well-heeled ones) at other times. The 112 plantation-style rooms range from vast to palatial and rack rates start from US$1200 per night in low season and become stratospheric in the winter high season. Golf has always been a big thing at Sandy Lane, and there are three courses; the hotel has a desalination plant for watering the greens and fairways and keeping the five man-made lakes full. The **Old Nine** nine-hole course dates from 1961 and the two newer 18-hole courses, **Country Club** and **Green Monkey**, were designed by Tom Fazio. If you can't afford to stay, an opportunity to see the place is to go and eat there; but you have to book ahead to get past the gate. The two main restaurants both have a great reputation and are in stunning open-air beachfront locations. Pillared and romantic L'Ajacou offers fine dining, while the more informal **Bajan Blue** is known for its afternoon tea and indulgent buffets, including a Sunday brunch; it also offers pizzas and sushi.

Market every Sunday in the grounds (see page 94), and, every March, the popular and excellent performing arts festival, **Holders Season** ⓘ *www.holdersseason.com*, see Festivals, page 13.

Holetown in St James, the island's third-largest town, boasts a large selection of restaurants, nightlife and shopping. Today it's a thoroughly modern town but it was originally named Jamestown, after King James I of England, and is the place where Captain John Powell landed in 1925 and claimed the island for England. Two years later, on 17 February 1627, his brother Captain Henry Powell landed with a party of 80 settlers and 10 slaves. The Holetown monument commemorates these events although it gives the incorrect date. A secondary plaque correctly marks the 350th anniversary of the first permanent settlement in 1627. The settlement was, until 1629, the island's only town, and it had the first fort and first governor's house. Holetown acquired its name because of the offloading and cleaning of ships in the very small tidal channel near the beach known as the 'hole'. After Lord Carlisle gained control of Barbados as a protectorate of The Crown, he decided to found his own settlement, which became Bridgetown, in the southern part of the island.

Sights

There is public beach access down paths near the post office and the police station on the main road (parking is behind the police station and bus stops are along Highway 1). The sand is swept every morning while the early risers are jogging or walking their dogs along the West Coast Boardwalk (a concrete path along the beachfront), and beach operators offer a range of watersports as well as sun lounger and umbrella rental. Holetown is overloaded with restaurants and bars and even with a two-week stay here you'd be pushed to try them all. Most of them are along First Street and Second Street – the first two streets to be built in Barbados and today the main nightlife area on the west coast.

Holetown provides the main shopping outside Bridgetown. On Highway 1 at the junction with First Street is the **Limegrove Lifestyle Centre** ⓘ *T620 5463, www.limegrove. com, Mon-Sat 1000-1900, Sun 1100-1800*, an attractive and upscale four-storey complex built around three open-air courtyards, which has luxury designer outlets, art galleries, restaurants, a cinema complex ⓘ *daily 1000-2200*, a spa and a fashionable central courtyard bar, The Lime Bar (see page 92). On the main road, the older **West Coast Mall Stores Shopping Centre** ⓘ *T419 3110, Mon-Sat 0800-2000, Sun 0900-1400*, has a large Massy Stores Supermarket, a branch of Cave Shepherd for duty-free items, and many other shops. Just south of West Coast Mall and set in lovely tropical gardens is the **Chattel Village** ⓘ *T432 4691, Mon-Sat 0900-1700, Sun 0930-1300*, a group of replica traditional fretwork chattel houses, all brightly painted, containing boutiques selling handicrafts, souvenirs and beachwear, a gourmet food shop and a couple of cafés. During the Holetown Festival in February (see page 13), the roadside along this stretch of Highway 1 is crammed with people attracted by an open-air market for arts and crafts, helped along with tempting local food and drink, while the road itself becomes a parade ground.

St James Parish Church ⓘ *Highway 1, north end of town, over the bridge on the left, T422 4117, www.stjames.truepath.com. Mon-Fri 0900-1300, Sun services 0715, 0800, 0900*. This, the oldest church on the island, was presumed to be established when the first settlers arrived in Holetown in 1627. However, the exact date of the original church is not clear although records held by the British Museum state that 'The Hole Church' in Barbados

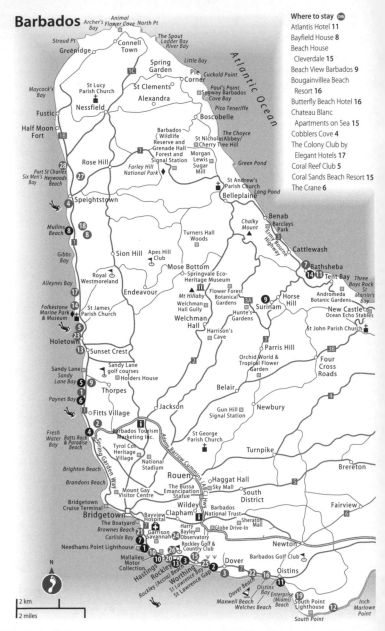

Barbados

Archer's Bay
Animal Flower Cave
North Pt
Stroud Pt
Greenidge
Connell Town
The Spout
Ladder Bay
River Bay
Little Bay
Spring Garden
Pie Corner
Cuckold Point
Paul's Point
Segway Barbados
Cove Bay
St Clements
Alexandra
Pico Teneriffe
Maycock's Bay
St Lucy Parish Church
Nessfield
Fustic
Boscobelle
Half Moon Fort
Rose Hill
Barbados Wildlife Reserve and Grenade Hall Forest and Signal Station
St Nicholas Abbey/ Cherry Tree Hill
The Choyce
Morgan Lewis Sugar Mill
Green Pond
Port St Charles
Six Men's Bay
Heywoods Beach
Speightstown
Farley Hill National Park
St Andrew's Parish Church
Belleplaine
Long Pond
Benab
Barclays Park
Mullins Beach
Gibbs Bay
Turners Hall Woods
Chalky Mount
Emy Bourne Highway
Cattlewash
Bathsheba
Tent Bay
Three Boys Rock
St Martin's Bay
Alleynes Bay
Sion Hill
Apes Hill Club
Mose Bottom
Springvale Eco-Heritage Museum
Mt Hillaby
Flower Forest Botanical Gardens
Welchman Hall Gully
Hunte's Gardens
Surinam
Horse Hill
Andromeda Botanic Gardens
New Castle
Ocean Echo Stables
Royal Westmoreland
Endeavour
Welchman Hall
Harrison's Cave
St John Parish Church
Folkestone Marine Park & Museum
St James Parish Church
Holetown
Sunset Crest
Parris Hill
Orchid World & Tropical Flower Garden
Four Cross Roads
Sandy Lane
Sandy Lane golf courses
Holders House
Sandy Lane Bay
Thorpes
Belair
Paynes Bay
Fitts Village
Jackson
Gun Hill Signal Station
Newbury
Fresh Water Bay
Batts Rock & Paradise Beach
Spring Garden Way
Barbados Tourism Marketing Inc.
Tyrol Cot Heritage Village
St George Parish Church
Turnpike
Brereton
Brighton Beach
National Stadium
Rouen
Haggat Hall
South District
Fairview
Brandons Beach
Mount Gay Visitor Centre
The Bussa Emancipation Statue
Sky Mall
Bridgetown Cruise Terminal
Bridgetown
Wildey
Clapham
Barbados National Trust
Sheraton Mall
Globe Drive-In
Newton
Bayview Hospital
The Boatyard
Browes Beach
Garrison Savannah
Harry Bayley Observatory
Rockley Golf & Country Club
Barbados Golf Club
Carlisle Bay
Needhams Point Lighthouse
Mallalieu Motor Collection
Hastings
Rockley
Worthing
Dover
Oistins
Barbados Golf Club
Rockley (Accra) Beach
St Lawrence Gap
St Lawrence Bay
Dover Beach
Oistins Bay
Enterprise (Miami) Beach
South Point Lighthouse
Inch Marlowe Point
Maxwell Beach
Welches Beach
South Point

2 km
2 miles

N

had been in existence well before 1668; there are also references to the church made in both 1629 and 1660. It is known that the original wooden building was destroyed by a hurricane in 1675 and was replaced by a light coral stone structure in 1680. In 1874 columns and arches were added and the nave roof raised. You can see the original baptismal font (1684) under the belfry, and in the north porch is the original bell of 1696. Many of the original settlers are buried here (although the oldest tombstone of William Balston who died in 1659 is in the Barbados Museum). There are several photos of registers, with many deaths attributed to the small pox epidemic of 1695-1696. The lovely stained-glass window depicting the Ascension was dedicated in 1924 in memory of the fallen in the First World War. On the front pew is a plaque to the ex-President of the USA Ronald Reagan and his wife Nancy, who worshipped here on Easter Sunday in 1982.

Folkestone Marine Park and Museum
ⓘ *Highway 1, opposite St James Parish Church, T422 2314. Daily 0900-1700, free entry.* This marine park stretches 2 km from Sandy Lane Bay in the south to the area known as Church Point; **Dottin's Reef** lies just offshore and is enclosed by buoys for snorkelling. The reef is not in pristine condition but it is surprisingly rewarding as there are quite a lot of fish and other marine life such as sea anemones, sea lilies, corals and sponges and you may see hawksbill turtles. Further offshore there is an artificial reef created in 1978 by the sinking of the Greek freighter *SS Stavronikita*, which rests under 36 m of water and is now home to numerous schooling large fish and corals. Because of its depth, and the fact that it is large enough for divers to get lost inside, the *Stavronikita* is classed an intermediate- to experienced-level dive (for Dive operators, see page 95). The beach is not great at Folkestone but it is always crowded with people taking advantage

of the safe swimming and snorkelling in the cordoned-off sea. Weekends are busy with families bringing enormous picnics and barbecues, cheerfully setting up home around a picnic bench. For around US$25 per person, glass-bottomed boats take you over the reef to two smaller wrecks further down the coast. The small two-roomed **museum** features displays and a photographic exhibit on marine life. Other facilities include a basketball court, children's playground, snack bar, toilets, showers, changing rooms with lockers and lifeguards; snorkelling gear can be hired. If you come by car there is a good shady car park, but you can also walk along the beachfront from Holetown, partly on the sand and partly on the West Coast Boardwalk.

East of Holetown

some varied outdoor excursions including a fantastic botanical garden

East of Holetown there is a clutch of attractions either side of Highway 2, also easily reachable from Bridgetown. Many of those listed below are in close proximity to each other in the island's central hillier and cooler parishes of St Thomas, St Joseph and St Andrew, and make a pleasant day trip away from the beach.

★Welchman Hall Gully

Welchman Hall, St Thomas, off Highway 2, T438 6671, www.welchmanhallgullybarbados.com. Daily 0900-1600, last entry 1530, Nov-Apr free guided tour Mon-Fri at 1030, other guided tours available with 24 hrs' notice. US$12, children (5-12) US$6, under 5s free.

Welchman Hall Tropical Forest Reserve, more commonly referred to as the Welchman Hall Gully, is in St Thomas, one of the hilliest parishes in Barbados. The gully was formed by the collapsed roofs of caves and is a fascinating 30- to 45-minute walk through one of the deep ravines that are so characteristic of this part of Barbados. You are at the edge of the limestone cap which covers most of the island to a depth of about 100 m. Owned by the Barbados National Trust, a good path leads for about 1.2 km through six sections, each with a slightly

Tip...

To get to Welchman Hall Gully from Bridgetown, Transport Board buses go from the Princess Alice Bus Terminal or private buses from Lower Green Terminal, all going to Sturges; the former drop you at the back of the gully, leaving you with a 1-km walk, the latter drop you nearer the entrance. The same buses will drop off at Harrison's Cave 1.4 km before the gully.

different theme. The first section has a devil tree, a stand of bamboo and a judas tree. Next you will go through jungle, which has lots of creepers, the 'pop-a-gun' tree and bearded fig clinging to the cliff (note the stalactites and stalagmites); a section devoted to palms and ferns: golden, silver, Macarthur and cohune palms, nutmegs and wild chestnuts; to open areas with tall leafy mahogany trees, rock balsam and mango trees. At the end of the walk are ponds with lots of frogs and toads. Best of all though is the wonderful view to the east coast. On the left are some steps leading to a gazebo, at the same level as the tops of the cabbage (Royal) palms. Look out for green monkeys; which are very likely to make an appearance thanks to banana feeding between 1030 and 1200. Entry fee to Welchman Hall Gully includes a booklet that lists over 50 plants and trees and there are clear and informative signs along the walk. There's a children's playground with a treehouse, mini zip-liner and rope swing, and the **Chunky Monkey Café** serves snacks and drinks including coconut water and rum punch.

Harrison's Cave

Allen View, St Thomas, off Highway 2, T417 3700, www.harrisonscave.com. Daily 1-hr train tours 0845-1545. US$30, children (under 12) US$15; book in advance for the 4-hr adventure tour (through the caves with knee pads and headlamps), daily 0900 and 1200, US$101, no children under 16; and the 1½-hr walk-in guided cave tour on foot, Sat 1600 and 1630, US$20, children US$10. Other tours include a scenic gully tour, junior explorer's tour and junior explorer's bat programme.

Welchman Hall Gully is connected geologically to nearby Harrison's Cave, about 1.4 km to the south. This little tourist trap has an impressive visitor centre with restaurant (fair), shop and a small display of local geology and Amerindian artefacts. You are first shown an interesting video of Barbados' geology, then taken into the limestone cave on an electric 'train'. The visit takes about an hour and you will see some superbly lit stalactites and stalagmites, waterfalls and large underground lakes. Be prepared to get a bit wet as the caves drip. There is a guide to point out the interesting formations and two stops for photo opportunities.

If you take Highway 2 heading to Bridgetown you will pass **Jack-in-the-Box Gully**, part of the same complex of Welchman Hall Gully and Harrison's Cave. **Coles Cave** (an 'undeveloped' cave that can easily be explored with a waterproof torch/flashlight) lies at its north end.

Mount Hillaby

About 2 km northeast of Welchman Hall Gully via Canefield Road, is Mount Hillaby, or Hillabys as it is affectionately called by Barbadians, the highest point on the island at a modest 337 m. It lies in the Scotland District in the parish of St Andrew, although the village of Hillaby borders St Andrew and St Thomas. It's not a pointy-topped mountain, more of an extended ridge of about 4 km. A narrow and pretty winding road goes up from the village though cattle farms and sugar cane fields to the top, where a small trail and steps into the bush lead to a concrete summit marker. If you visit Mount Hillaby early in the morning you'll most likely see the area covered in an enchanting mist. Later in the day the mist clears to reveal broad views of the lush countryside to the northeast coast. To reach the village from the west or south, go via Highway 2A and then Duke's Road.

★ Flower Forest Botanical Gardens

Richmond, St Joseph, T433 8152, www.flowerforestbarbados.com. Daily 0800-1600. US$15, children (4-12) US$7.50, under 4s free. To get there turn off Highway 2 on the Melvin Hill road just after the agricultural station and follow the signs.

Just under 3 km north of Welchman Hall Gully and at 270 m above sea level is this 21-ha (53-acre) beautifully landscaped botanical garden on a former sugar plantation. Named paths wend their way around the hillside; they are well maintained and even suitable for wheelchairs, although there are a few which go off the beaten track and can only be negotiated on foot. The garden contains species not only from Barbados but from all over the world, all beautifully arranged

Tip...
A good map/information sheet is provided for a self-guided tour, umbrellas are available if it's drizzly, and there's a pleasant café for lunches and teas.

with plenty of colour year-round. You can find heliconias, ginger lilies, orchids, anthurium, ixoras and bougainvillea as well as productive plants such as bananas, cocoa, coffee and breadfruit. The outstanding feature of this garden, however, is the forest. Enormous trees loom above you, with Royal and other palms giving shade to the paths, while in between you can find bearded fig trees, huge baobab and mango trees. Here and there they open onto large grassy areas affording excellent views over the valley to the east coast. **Liv's Lookout** in particular has a fantastic outlook all up the northeast seaboard. To the west you can see Mount Hillaby (see page 53).

Springvale Eco-Heritage Museum

Springvale, Highway 2, St Andrew, T438 7011. Mon-Sat 1000-1500, Sun by appointment. US$5 per person.

Springvale is an 80-ha (200-acre) former sugar plantation and the manager's house has been converted into a museum of rural Barbadian life. It is very low key and informal, and worth a detour if you are in the area. The owner, Newlands Greenidge, can trace his ancestry back to 1631 and a ship which came from Greenwich. He will explain the day-to-day items in the museum, which include antique furniture and old-time cooking and household utensils, showing how people lived in colonial times. He will also take you along a path outside leading to a stream through groves of bananas, coconuts and bamboo, pointing out the various plants and their uses. The café serves local juices and food according to what is in season.

Hunte's Gardens

Castle Grant, Highway 3A, St Joseph, T433 3333, www.huntesgardensbarbados.com. Daily 0900-1600, closed mid-May to mid-Jun (to take part in the UK's Chelsea Flower Show). US$15 per person.

Along Highway 3A at Castle Grant is another treat for keen gardeners, Hunte's Gardens, which can easily be combined with visits to Welchman Hall Gully and the Flower Forest Botanical Gardens. Genial host, horticulturist Anthony Hunte, has lovingly created this rainforest garden in a gully, with flowering plants growing in a variety of habitats, from sunny, open spaces to a dark sink hole. A pretty path winds its way through a series of little gardens tucked away in private areas with strategically placed benches where you can pause to admire the view and watch the birds and butterflies. At the end you are welcomed back to the veranda of the house for a rum punch or fruit juice (and an entertaining chat with the owner if he's there).

The coastal Highway 1 runs north from Holetown on to Speightstown in the parish of St Peter and 22 km north of Bridgetown. This is the second largest town on the island and the bus terminus for the north, but, with a population of less than 4000, it retains a village atmosphere with sidewalk vendors selling fresh fruit and vegetables and fishermen unloading their catch along the jetty. It is a lively place during opening hours, but dead the rest of the time. Pronounced Spikestown (or Spikestong), it is named after William Speight, a merchant and member of the Governor Hawley's first House of Assembly. An important port in the early days, it was known as Little Bristol, because of its trade with Bristol, England and it used to have four jetties. It also had three forts, no longer in evidence: Orange Fort, Coconut Fort and Denmark Fort, while outside town were Dover Fort and Heywoods Battery. They didn't see a lot of action but the town was once invaded by Oliver Cromwell's forces when Barbados remained loyal to King Charles I. Colonel Alleyne led the Roundheads ashore in December 1651 only to be shot dead by Royalists. His forces captured the town, their only victory, and a peace treaty was later signed at Oistins.

Sights
Speightstown has some interesting old buildings, once-grand townhouses that belonged to the wealthy merchants, and many two-storey shops with Georgian balconies and overhanging galleries. Sadly many have been knocked down by passing lorries and a fire in 1941 destroyed almost everything near the bridge on the ocean side of **Queen's Street**. This area was replaced with the **Speightstown Esplanade**, a pleasant waterfront with a stage area and wooden bench seating for outdoor events, and a tremendous view along the town's coastline and beaches to the south. Just south of the Esplanade is the **Speightstown Fish Market** (flying fish is one of the most popular catches, but also look out for marlin, king fish, mahi mahi, swordfish and tuna; ask the vendors what's in season). Alongside the fish market's long jetty is the characterful, if not slightly ramshackle, rum shop-style **Fisherman's Pub** (see page 89), which has a great view of the sea from the terrace and is a popular local watering hole and lunch stop for tourists on island tours.

Arlington House Museum ① *Queen's St, T422 4064, www.barbadosnationaltrust.org. Mon-Fri 0900-1700, Sat 0900-1500. US$12.50, children (6-17) US$6.25, under 6s free.* Arlington House is a 17th-century 'single house', meaning it's the width of a single room. It is believed to have been the prototype for the Charleston Single, common in Charleston, South Carolina, but is the last remaining example on Barbados. It tapers towards the back and the ground-floor room was once believed to have been a chandler's, as the original owners, the Skinners, owned one of the town's jetties. There is a separate entrance to the first-floor room and above that there is a second floor with a balcony, the main living quarters for the family and, above that again, an attic with gabled windows that was probably used for sleeping and storage. The house was built of coral, limestone and rubble masonry, all cemented together with a mortar made from egg whites and molasses creating walls that are over two feet thick. It has been beautifully renovated by the Barbados National Trust as the Arlington House Museum with audiovisual displays, including videos of interviews with members of the local community. It's very engaging and and exhibits are well arranged under three subjects: **Speightstown Memories** introduces the lives of the island's first settlers; **Plantation Memories** illustrates the influence of colonization, the plantation system and the sugar cane industry on the island; and **Wharf Memories** recalls the importance of Speightstown as a leading port and trade hub.

St Peter's Parish Church ① *Orange St, T422 3599, www.stpeter.anglican.bb. Mon-Fri 1000-1800, Sat 1000-1300, Sun services 0730, 0915, 1900.* First built of timber in 1629, then again in 1665, St Peter's was rebuilt once more in 1837 in early Georgian style with an impressive square bell tower and ramparts. The architecture was strongly associated with the number seven, relating to the seven days of Creation in Genesis I: there are seven windows to the north and south, seven columns in the interior, the roof is divided into seven parts and the stained-glass window has seven sections. A fire in 1980 destroyed the roof and floors, although the fine eastern stained-glass window and the walls survived. The church was restored in 1983.

Tip...

St Peter's Parish Church's Annual Flower and Garden Festival is a five-day event held every January, when the best floral arrangers of the island showcase their talent and the church is decorated with blooms such as anthuriums, heliconias and orchids (check the website or Facebook page for details).

The Speightstown Mural An unusual attraction in town is a mural depicting the history of Barbados in its many phases. Privately commissioned in 2013 by restauranteur Pierre Spenard, it is on the north wall of Jordan's Supermarket between the seafront and Queen's Street. It measures 21 m by 7.5 m, was painted by John Pugh, of California, and Don Small, of Barbados, and took 18 months to complete. The detail is fantastic and the longer you look at it the more you see of the people and events that have created modern Barbados. Scenes of Harrison's Cave blend seamlessly into historical scenes of the raising of the Barbados flag at Independence, while green monkeys merge with chattel houses and the original Amerindian inhabitants of the island.

Mullins Beach and Gibbes Beach This 275-m-long stretch of soft white sand is just south of Speightstown off Highway 1. It shelves gently into usually calm water and has roped off-areas for snorkelling and swimming. As well as a large car park, there are sun loungers and umbrellas for hire, plenty of shady trees, and vendors offering watersports, although there are no changing facilities or lifeguards. There has been some erosion of the beach but it is still a lovely place to come for the day. A shack behind the beach sells beer, rum and ice creams, while **Mullins Beach Bar** (see page 89) is a great spot to watch the sun set. Immediately south of Mullins Beach is Gibbes Beach, another entirely un-commercialized arc of pristine sand, backed by soaring trees and some of the most desirable villas on the island. If you're willing to get your legs wet, you can sometimes reach Gibbes by walking around from Mullins (it depends on the tide); otherwise it's a tricky track through the villa properties down from Highway 1B.

North of Speightstown

A glitzy 9-ha (22-acre) marina has been built at Heywoods Beach just north of Speightstown. Known as **Port St Charles** ① *T419 1000, www.portstcharles.com*, it is a huge and impenetrable development with a massive wall around the outside to deter casual visitors. It is also an official port of entry into Barbados with coastguard, police and immigration on site for entry by yacht or helicopter. Arranged around a small inland man-made lagoon, there are 145 residential villas, condos and apartments, a yacht club, heliport and watersports as well as berths for around 140 yachts including six super-yachts (up to 250 ft in length). Water taxis scoot around the lagoon taking residents to the various facilities on site or on shopping trips to Speightstown. Most of the apartments and villas are privately owned, but some are available for short-term holiday rental. Public access to Heywoods Beach is off Highway 1B between the all-inclusive **Almond Beach Resort** and Port St Charles, where there is a small road and parking. The water here is calm and good for swimming and snorkelling and there are some small rock-enclosed pools that are perfect for children to wade in.

Immediately north of Port St Charles, Highway 1B passes through Six Men's fishing village on the bay of the same name, where the beach is picturesque but has mixed sea conditions and some undertow; it is mostly used by local fishermen serving the tiny fish market. Divers though may want to explore the *Pamir*, a 165-ft wreck of a freighter that was scuttled in 1985 to create an artificial reef that lies only 30 m offshore in **Six Men's Bay**. Easily accessible by boat or swimming from shore, and with many large holes in its hull, it's a popular spot for first-time wreck divers.

North of Six Men's, Highway 1B turns inland towards the parish of St Lucy in the north of the island, while the **Sherman Hall Moon Fort** coastal road, lined with simple chattel houses, is generally quiet, except when buses come whizzing through. The unkempt sandy beach along this stretch has a certain charm but backs on to the road and can be narrow at high tide; there are rocks underwater and it is predominantly used for hauling up fishing boats. Nevertheless, around the village of Sherman are a clutch of exclusive villas and the **Little Good Harbour** hotel, where **The Fish Pot**, one of the best restaurants on this part of the coast, is a good spot for lunch, see page 89.

North
coast

Far from the crowds and the bustle of the west and south coasts, the northern tip of Barbados in the parish of St Lucy has a rugged and picturesque landscape of dramatic coral limestone cliffs, jagged rock formations, and quiet, isolated bays. The true 'north' begins after Port St Charles, and soon you leave behind the development of the west coast strip and emerge into proper countryside as Highway 1B veers inland. Narrow roads lead off to the coast. The Atlantic Ocean can be rough and wild and huge waves crash into cliffs, creating tunnels, caves, platforms and enormous jacuzzis. Round the tip on the eastern side there are some lovely shingle coves to explore, favourite picnic spots but otherwise deserted. Swimming is possible at low tide, but be cautious, and take local advice about which places are safe and which have dangerous currents. The northeastern part of the country is known as the Scotland District for its rugged appearance and similarities perceived by the first colonizers. Although the landscape doesn't match the majesty of the Scottish Highlands, it has its own charms and there are some interesting places to explore.

Animal Flower Cave
North Point, St Lucy, off Highway 1C, T439 8797, www.animalflowercave.com. Daily 0900-1630. US$10, children (5-12) US$5, under 5s free; restaurant 1100-1500.

Located on the rugged and ragged clifftops of the northernmost point of the island is this expansive cave, one of many caverns created by the pounding waves of the Atlantic, with its mouth above the sea when it is calm. The 'animals' are sea anemones but, while they were seemingly in abundance when the cave was discovered and named in the 1700s, they are rarely seen today. A stairway through a blow-hole in the bedrock provides access, and guides will walk you through several huge chambers filled with beautiful rock formations, some of them tinted by the oxidation of copper and iron, and take you to rock 'windows' just above the level of the sea. The floor of the cave is very stony and can be slippery, so wear good shoes, and bring swimwear and a towel as there is a totally transparent and absolutely still pool in one chamber where you can swim looking out to sea. The view from North Point over the cliffs and ledges is dramatic and well worth the trip even if (or particularly when) the cave is shut because of high seas. There are a number of craft stalls here and a reasonable restaurant and bar.

> **Tip...**
> Buses from Bridgetown go via the west coast and Speightstown to Connell Town on Highway 1C; tell the driver to drop you at the end of 'Cave Gap' and from there it's a 10-minute walk along Animal Flower Cave Road.

Ladder Bay and River Bay
Rounding the northern tip of the island, you will find several remote coastal areas to visit: Ladder Bay, River Bay, Little Bay and Cove Bay. Some of these coarse sandy coves, popular with Barbadians for picnics at the weekend but otherwise completely deserted, are only accessible along tracks. There are good walks along the cliffs around here; for instance from Ladder Bay to River Bay and on to Little Bay along the Antilles Flat. But beware, as the ground is rocky and there is no shade; wear sturdy shoes and sun protection.

The abandoned and now-ruined North Point Surf Resort at **Ladder Bay** is off Highway 1C,. Park outside the wall, from where you can walk around the **Spout**, a geyser-like 30-m-high water spurt courtesy of a spectacular blowhole, and a small, rather dangerous beach. Just south, at **River Bay**, there's a shallow, calm spot to take a dip while the Atlantic rages a few metres beyond. It has a public changing facility with showers and toilets, and is served by the odd bus from Connell Town; an option here would be to combine a visit with the Animal Flower Cave and walk between the two (which takes about an hour) and then catch a bus from either side.

Little Bay
If you drive inland from Ladder Bay and then through **Spring Garden**, you'll re-emerge on the coast at Little Bay near the village of **Pie Corner**. There is a quiet beach here with golden sand and limestone cliffs, usually unoccupied unless a tour group stops by. The sea here is far too perilous for swimming, but on the north edge of the bay there's a ledge of rock protecting a completely circular and calm natural pool that is just deep enough to swim in. Pick your way over the jagged rocks carefully and wear shoes. You can also climb up the cliffs overlooking Little Bay for a good view of the north coast's spectacular blowholes.

Cove Bay

A bit further south and in a peaceful, rural setting, Cove Bay (also called Gay's Cove), is a popular picnic area and very scenic. It's not easy to get to and while you can drive to the cliffs overlooking the bay, the track goes through a field of cows, goats and blackbelly sheep. It is easy to get bogged down so if the ground looks wet, park further back on Cove Bay Road and walk the last kilometre or so. From the clifftop vantage point you get a good view of the semi-circllular bay below (it's a bit of a scramble to get down to the shingle beach itself), and beyond it to the 80-m-high **Pico Teneriffe**, a large rock on top of a steeply sloping cliff. The whole of the coast to Bathsheba is visible too, lined with the foam of breaking Atlantic waves.

Back on Cove Bay Road, **Segway Barbados** ① *T253 6772, www.segwaybarbados.com*, offers guided off-road Segway tours along the northeast coastline between Cove Bay and Little Bay (you must make a reservation). The three daily tours (at 0945, 1145 and 1345) last approximately 1½ hours after a little bit of training; US$75, children (10-15) US$65, no under 10s, minimum weight 36 kg, maximum weight 120 kg. Helmets and water are provided, and there's a glass of rum punch at the end of the excursion. Take sunscreen and wear sturdy shoes. It's loads of fun, the route goes across fields of grazing cows and blackbelly sheep and along farm tracks with plenty of stops along the clifftops to enjoy the tremendous views. Transport can be arranged (and they pick up groups from Bridgetown Cruise Terminal most mornings when cruise ships are in port).

Inland from the north coast

a great house, sugar plantations and indigenous island wildlife

Just inland from the northeast coast are a group of attractions that are fairly close to one another and are easily accessed via Highway 2A from Bridgetown and the west coast or Highway 2 from the east coast. Spanning the parishes of St Peter and St Andrew, this region is the hilliest area of Barbados and there are plenty of views across to the coast and the Scotland District.

★St Nicholas Abbey

Cherry Tree Hill, St Peter, T422 5357, www.stnicholasabbey.com. Sun-Fri 1000-1530. US$20, children (5-11) US$10, under 5s free.

St Nicholas Abbey is on a 162-ha (400-acre) estate comprising 91 ha (225 acres) of sugar cane fields as well as lush tropical gullies, mahogany forests, formal gardens and **Cherry Tree Hill** (260 m), a prominent landmark that you can walk or drive up. If you're going south and inland from Cove Bay it's just under 4 km via Boscobelle; other routes to the abbey from the west coast and the south go via Highway 2A; there are plenty of signposts.

Approached down a long and impressive avenue of mahogany trees, St Nicholas Abbey was never actually an abbey – it has no monks' cells or cloisters and some have supposed that the 'St' and 'Abbey' were added to impress. It is, however, one of only three surviving Jacobean mansions in the western hemisphere (the other two are Drax Hall, also in Barbados in St George near the centre of the island, the first place on the island where sugar was cultivated in the 1640s and today a private residence; and Bacon's Castle in rural Virginia in the US, which, like Barbados, was a wealthy English plantation colony in the 17th century). St Nicholas Abbey is thought to have been built by Colonel Benjamin

Beringer in 1658, but was sold to Sir John Yeamans, who set out from Speightstown in 1663 to colonize South Carolina. The three-storeyed house has a façade with three ogee-shaped Dutch gables over its main portico and cornerstone chimneys and fireplaces of local coral stone; as these are unnecessary in the Caribbean it's likely that Beringer purchased the plans in England.

Tip...
Allow about two hours to explore St Nicholas Abbey and the estate, starting no later than 1430 as visitors must leave the property by 1615.

Today, scrupulously restored, it is one of the architectural treasures of Barbados, with a Chippendale staircase and cedar-panelled rooms containing antique furnishings including a 1759 James Thwaite of London grandfather clock, an 1810 Coalport dinner service and a collection of early Wedgwood portrait medallions. Visitors are given an interesting tour of the ground floor of the house, as well as the rum and sugar museum and the gardens. The rum distillery uses a traditional pot-still to make the unique St Nicholas Abbey Rum sold in the shop, which also sells molasses and brown sugar from the estate, plus jellies and chutneys made with fruit from the gardens. Behind the house, near the 400-year-old sandbox tree, the Terrace Café serves lunch, tea and other light refreshments.

From the top of Cherry Tree Hill there are glorious views all over the Scotland District, which falls mainly within the parish of St Andrew. It is believed that cherry trees grew here once, but today the road up the hill is lined with mahogany trees.

Morgan Lewis Sugar Mill
Morgan Lewis, St Peter, T422 7429. Daily 0900-1700. Free.

At the bottom of Cherry Tree Hill, about 2.5 km from the abbey, the Morgan Lewis Windmill was built around 1776 and was the last working sugar windmill in Barbados; it stopped operating in 1947 and in 1962 was given to the Barbados National Trust. The mill consists of a tower, four giant arms, gears that transfer the turning of the sails to the turning of the rollers, housing on top, and a 33-m tail that connects the housing to the ground. By moving the tail, the whole apparatus can be rotated to face the direction of the prevailing wind. With all the equipment still intact, it is believed to be the largest and only complete sugar windmill surviving in the whole of the Caribbean; sadly, it hasn't functioned since lightning struck the tower in 2007. Until it is repaired, visitors can walk around the base to take photos, and it is often open as part of the Barbados National Trust's Open House Programme (see box, page 18). On the flat savannah at the bottom of the hill is a cricket pitch, a pleasant place to watch the game at weekends.

Barbados Wildlife Reserve and Grenade Hall Forest and Signal Station
Farley Hill, Highway 2, St Peter, T422 8826, www.barbadoswildlifereserve.com. Daily 1000-1700, US$11.75, children (3-12) US$5.90, under 3s free.

This family attraction off Highway 2 occupies 1.6 ha (4 acres) near the top of Farley Hill, next to the Grenade Hall Signal Forest and Signal Station. It was first established by a Canadian primatologist in 1982 for the conservation and study of green monkeys, which arrived on Barbados in the 17th century on slave ships from West Africa and are now widespread on the island. Short paths meander through the mahogany forest, where banana trees and other fruit and vegetables are planted to feed the animals. Some are steep and quite uneven, but if you look closely at the bricks, you can still see the stamps of the British manufacturing companies; the bricks were brought to Barbados as ballast on ships during the 17th and 18th centuries and used to construct boiler furnaces in sugar factories; now they have been recycled as these pathways.

Animals seen roaming all over the paths include the bushy-tailed mongoose, peacocks, guinea fowl, iguanas and the large red-footed Barbados tortoise, while brocket deer and agouti lounge in the shade to escape the heat. The caged birds and reptiles are less impressive (the parrots particularly seem frustrated). It is, however, an excellent place to see green monkeys close up if they haven't taken off to the forest next door. The best time to come (especially for children) is for the 1400 feeding when staff bring out wheelbarrows of fruit, the monkeys return and other animals gather expectantly. Try to be quiet, so as not to disturb them. A café and shop at the reception area sell snacks, drinks and gifts.

The entry fee to the reserve also covers Grenade Hall Forest and Signal Station, next door, where winding shaded pathways with interpretative signs have been laid out through the whitewood, dogwood, mahogany and silk cotton trees; some are steep and slippery so watch your footing. The Signal Station (1819) was one of six erected at strategic points across the island for communication using flags or semaphores (to warn of such things as approaching ships or slave rebellions). Today it has been restored and an audio guide gives the history with sound effects. The wonderful panoramic views give you a good idea of its original role in the communications network.

Farley Hill National Park
Farley Hill, Highway 2, St Peter, T422 3555. Daily 0830-1730. Free for pedestrians, US$3 per car to park.

On the other side of the road from the wildlife reserve and set in a pleasant park popular with Barbadian families for Sunday picnics is the atmospheric ruin of Farley Hill House. Building began in 1818, with additional rooms being added over the next 50 years. It eventually grew to be regarded as the most impressive mansion on Barbados and in the mid-19th century the property was owned by Sir Graham Briggs, a wealthy British planter and legislator, who improved both the house and gardens, importing many plants and trees onto the island. It was used as the location for the 1957 film *Island in the Sun* – the story of a love affair across racial boundaries, starring Harry Belafonte and Joan Fontaine. Sadly, in 1965, a disastrous fire destroyed the house's interior and roof, and only the solid stone walls survived. It was purchased by the government and was opened as a national park by Queen Elizabeth II in 1966. Now, if you look through the mahogany trees and across a manicured lawn, you'll see the imposing Georgian stone façade pierced by great windows; benches have been set at strategic points so you can enjoy the breeze coming in off the Atlantic and the spectacular views over the Scotland District, right down to the lighthouse on **Ragged Point**. There are many imported and native tree species, some labelled, planted over 7 ha (17 acres) of woodland, and the forest is transformed into the stage for musical and theatrical events several times a year. It is also a popular venue for weddings.

Tip...

To get to Farley Hill for both the national park and the Barbados Wildlife Reserve and Grenade Hall Forest and Signal Station, take any bus along Highway 2 and get off at Benny Hall, Saint Peter; everything is signposted and the bus driver will tell you where to alight.

East
coast

Wild and windy, unspoilt and untamed, the Atlantic coast
has a raw energy and is stunningly beautiful. Craggy cliffs
form a backdrop for huge bays filled with boulders which
appear to have rolled down the hillsides into the foaming
surf. The strong currents and powerful waves make the
sea too dangerous for swimming – Barbadians say "the
sea ain't got no back door" – but you can wade and look
for sea creatures in the numerous rock pools and it is the
nearest place to heaven for surfers, who can be seen out
there at any time of day waiting for the right wave. Hiking
is also excellent, particularly along the abandoned railway
track which hugs the coastline. Some accommodation can
be found in Bathsheba, the main village, but otherwise
the east coast is sparsely inhabited, dotted only with
colourful villages of wooden chattel houses and banana
and coconut trees lining the roadsides.

Inland, but within easy reach of either the east or
west coast, are several stunning gardens and natural
attractions, such as ancient forests and caves.

Much of the East Coast Road, opened by Queen Elizabeth II on 15 February 1966, has today been renamed the Ermy Bourne Highway. It runs from a junction with Highway 2 at St Andrew's Parish Church near Belleplaine, south through Barclays Park and Cattlewash and down to Bathsheba. Here it joins Highway 3 that branches off both southwest to Bridgetown, and southeast through Bath to Codrington College and then beyond into the parish of St Philip. This drive, about 16 km from Belleplaine to the college, affords fine views of long beaches pounded by the Atlantic, while meadows tumble down from the hillsides into the ocean. Look out for grazing blackbelly sheep, which are commonly mistaken for goats.

St Andrew's Parish Church
Junction of Highway 2 and Ermy Bourne Highway, Belleplaine, St Andrew, T435 9097. Services Tue and Thu 0700, Sun 0800.

Just less than 3 km south of the Morgan Lewis Sugar Mill and 1 km before Bellepaine, this quaint but handsome English-style parish church on Highway 2 was first built of wood in 1630 and then reconstructed in stone in 1846 after being destroyed by a hurricane in 1831. It sits among lush casuarina trees and has a Gothic-style square tower and gallery running on three sides. Often locked except at service times, the grounds are lovely and the well-kept church with its white-painted gateposts, windows and gables is quite photogenic.

Turners Hall Woods
Isolation Rd, Cheltenham, St Andrew, just under 2 km west of Highway 2. Open 24 hrs. Free.

Inland and west of the Ermy Bourne Highway at Belleplaine are the 20-ha (50-acre) Turners Hall Woods. Although not well signposted (you may have to ask), they are reached by following Isolation Road; a distance of about 2.5 km from the highway. It is thought that these woods have changed little since the arrival of the English settlers, who stripped much of the island bare for planting sugar cane in the 17th century. There is a fairly steep main hiking trail of about 1.75 km, with several short secondary trails branching off to the left and right, and also a number of small streams and ponds flowing under the dense canopy of trees. At least 32 tree species have been identified, including silk cotton, sandbox, bulletwood, trumpet tree, locust, fustic and cabbage (Royal) palms. About 152 cm of rain falls annually in this area, so it's not classed as a true rainforest, despite the multi-layered tree canopy and the presence of lianas and ferns. But it can get very hot and humid in the forest so make sure you have plenty of drinking water.

Long Pond
Long Pond is a secluded coastal estuarine area about 1.5 km east of Belleplaine off Ermy Bourne Highway; you'll need to park at Windy Hill and scramble a couple of hundred metres through the sand dunes to get there. It's a shallow brackish-water lagoon separated from the sea at low tide by a sand bank, and is fed by Long

Tip...
To reach the east coast, buses to Bathsheba go across from Speightstown (45 minutes) on the west coast via Highway 2, Belleplaine and the Ermy Bourne Highway; and from Fairchild Street Bus Terminal in Bridgetown to Bathsheba (50 minutes) via Highway 3.

Pond River, one of the four rivers on the island. Thanks to crabs, tiny fish, shrimp and crustaceans, Long Pond is a habitat and foraging area for many shore and waterbirds including sandpipers, plovers and herons, and you may also see resident ospreys in the casuarina trees on the south bank of the lagoon. You can paddle in the lagoon, but watch the very soft mud beneath your feet.

Barclays Park and Chalky Mount

About 2 km south of Long Pond at Benab, 20-ha (50-acre) Barclays Park straddles Ermy Bourne Highway and stretches from a wide swathe of dark tan-coloured beach on one side up the hillside on the other. Access is free, and it is a good place to stop for a picnic under the shady casuarina trees; there is parking on either side of the highway. The land was given to the government of Barbados by Barclays Bank to commemorate independence in 1966 and the park was opened by Queen Elizabeth II. Above the park you can hike through meadows to the top of Chalky Mount for magnificent views of the east coast. It takes about 45 minutes to an hour, and if you ask locally for the exact path you are likely to be given several different routes. This 167-m-high hill of reddish-brown (not chalky) clay can be spotted from some distance away looming over the coast. Some people say it looks like the figure of a man resting with his hands over his stomach and it is also known locally as 'Napoleon'. In Chalky Mount Village (also accessed by road from the west side), generations of potters living mostly in wooden houses on the hillside used to make local cookware such as 'pepperpots' (to preserve meat) and 'monkeys' (a kind of water jug), although the practice has dwindled in recent years.

Cattlewash

On Ermy Bourne Highway between Barclays Park and Bathsheba, the beach at Cattlewash is a long expanse of sand and is perfect for an isolated beach walk; the reef pools exposed at low tide provide safe waters in which to bathe and cool off. There is a lifeguard station manned at busier times but no other facilities. The beach got its name from the farmers who used to take their cattle down to the sand bank and have them washed by the crashing waves to rid them of parasites. You can walk along the sand the 2 km from Cattlewash to Bathsheba.

★Bathsheba

Bathsheba is in the parish of St Joseph, about halfway up the east coast, and 19 km northeast of Bridgetown via Highway 3. It has a double bay with wave-eroded rocks and boulders at each end and in the middle. The beach is sandy but at the water's edge it turns to flat rocks, platforms interspersed with rock pools where you can cool off at low tide. Windswept and with pounding surf, swimmers confine themselves to these pools, best in the shelter of the enormous boulders (watch out for sea urchins), but Bathsheba is one of Barbados' top surfing beaches. The bay seems to be almost white as the surf trails out behind the Atlantic rollers. The popular surf spots are **Soup Bowl** and **Parlour**, where waves break consistently year-round but are best between September and November. Surfing championships are often held here. Bathsheba village is home to a small community of fishing folk and their families and is effectively just one long beach road, dotted with the odd rum shop; it's just about as laid-back as it gets in Barbados. If you're neither a surfer nor a tidal pool-paddler, then there are plenty of walks in the area. Low-key accommodation is available, and this is also where some Barbadians spend their weekends, with many owning holiday homes in the area.

Just south of Bathsheba (a suburb really), picturesque **Tent Bay** is home to a small fish market, and colourful local fishing boats can be seen making their way in and out of the

ON THE ROAD
East coast railway line

A railway was built in 1883 between Bridgetown and Belleplaine, up the east coast in St Andrew. It was built to transport sugar to the docks at Bridgetown for export, and also to afford Barbadians and visitors a luxurious trip to the east coast, where welcoming parties awaited them at hotels. The line had 98 bridges, severe curves and one of the steepest gradients of any railway in the world – the cutting at My Lady's Hole, near Conset Bay in St John is spectacular, with a gradient of 1:31. The railway had at its disposal five locomotives from England, named after the parishes through which the line ran. While the railway had some years of success, by the end of the 1800s it was plagued with many troubles. Firstly the train moved slowly, at an average speed of 6 miles (10 km) per hour, and had no washrooms; it is said that men could jump off the front of the train to relieve themselves, and jump back on the caboose afterwards. The railway took a beating from the Atlantic sea spray and from landslides and wave erosion, and the locomotives often slipped off the line; the crew would sprinkle sand on the track to get them back on again while the first-class passengers remained seated, the second-class walked and the third-class pushed. It continued to decay and by 1934 the service for passengers was discontinued; by 1937 the railway was shut down and the steel and tracks were removed altogether. Today there is good walking along the old railway line between Bathsheba and Bath.

bay in the morning and evening. Like the other beaches, there are strong currents and swimming is not recommended. The landmark **Atlantis Hotel** (see page 84) opened here in 1884 when the old railway between Bridgetown and Belleplaine (1881-1937; see box, page above) ran directly in front of the hotel and made a stop at the bottom of the steps. The **Atlantis** is still a great place for lunch on a tour of the island and is well known for its Bajan buffets, see page 89.

Up on the slopes behind Bathsheba is a dense 34-ha (85-acre) woodland known as **Joe's River Rain Forest**. Along with Turners Hall Woods, this is the only area on the island where the forests have remained largely intact since the English settlers arrived. It is full of mahogany trees, cabbage (Royal) palms, bearded fig trees and citrifolia; green monkeys and hummingbirds may be seen and there are nature trails and picnic areas. The woodland climbs up from the Atlantic coast to one of the highest points in Barbados known as **Hackleton's Cliff**, which provides yet another spectacular view of the east coast. On a clear day, this view can span from Pico Teneriffe in the north to Ragged Point in the southeast. It was allegedly named after a man called Hackleton who committed suicide by riding his horse over the cliff in the 17th century. At the top of the cliff are three burial vaults dating back to 1865 and containing the remains of the Hackleton, Forster, Cox and Culpepper families, some of the earliest settlers to arrive in Barbados. You can also drive up to the top from the west side; signposts on Highway 3 will take you via **Horse Hill** and up to **Hackleton's Cliff Lookout**.

Andromeda Botanic Gardens
Foster Hall, Bathsheba, St Joseph, T433 9384, www.andromedabarbados.com. Daily 0900-1630 last entry, but exit whenever you wish, US$15, children (under 12) free with paying adults, entrance fee covers unlimited visits within 3 weeks.

Perched up on the hillside with a fabulous view of the ocean is one of Barbados' prettiest gardens. It covers 2.5 ha (6 acres) above the bay at Bathsheba and is within walking distance of the beach (although it is uphill all the way – hot work). The garden started as a private plant collection around the home of Iris Bannochie (1914-1988), a leading

Tip...
Entry to Andromeda Botanic Gardens is free for UK members of the Royal Horticultural Society, and half price for members of the English and Scottish National Trusts.

expert on horticulture on the island who laid out trails in 1954 alongside a stream, now a prominent water feature, on land owned by her family since 1740. She bequeathed the gardens to the Barbados National Trust in 1988. The gardens contain plants from all over Barbados as well as species from other parts of the world, particularly Asia, amounting to over 600 in total. There are many varieties of orchid, heliconia, hibiscus and flowering trees and its blooms are regular winners at the Royal Horticultural Society's Chelsea Flower Show in London. You have a choice of two self-guided walks through immaculate gardens, sprawling over the hillside between limestone boulders – **Iris's Path** has more to see in the way of plants, while **John's Path** passes an astonishingly vast bearded fig tree. It is always full of interest and colour, with good explanatory leaflets for each walk, telling you of the uses of each plant as well as where to stop and rest. The **café** offers good food – Bajan fishcakes, sandwiches with home-made bread, salads, coffee, fresh juices and cakes – and is open until 1645, and there's also an **art gallery**.

St John Parish Church
Church View, St John, T433 5599, www.anglican.bb/~stjohn. Daily 0600-1800. Free but donations appreciated.

Around 5 km after Bathsheba on the way to Bath, turn off Highway 3 at New Castle and head inland for just over 2 km uphill to Church View and St John Parish Church (follow the road up from Martin's Bay on the coast). A classic solid Gothic church, it is in a magnificent location perched high up on a 240-m cliff with views over the Scotland District and the entire rugged east coast. The original church was probably built of wood around 1645, but it was destroyed by fire and was replaced in 1660 with a stone structure, which supposedly cost the diocese 110,000 lbs sugar. The building was badly damaged by the hurricane of 1675, and successive buildings were destroyed by hurricanes in 1780 and 1831. The present church (the fifth) was built is 1836; the chancel was added in 1876 and its beautiful stained-glass windows were added quite a bit later, in 1907. There is an interesting pulpit made from five different kinds of wood – ebony, mahogany, manchineel, locust oak and pine. You will also find the grave of Fernando Paleologus, a descendant of Emperor Constantine the Great, whose family was driven from the throne in Constantinople by the Turks. Fernando died in 1678, having been a resident here for over 20 years. There are some fine cabbage (Royal) palms in the churchyard, which is interesting to stroll around, but pick your moment: the church is on the itinerary for island tours and you may be jostling for space with the occupants of the latest cruise ship in port.

Martin's Bay
On the opposite side of Highway 3 and down a steep twisty hill, Martin's Bay is a pretty beach perched below green-palmed hills. A shallow reef breaks the waves and creates small pools perfect for paddling; further out are rougher waters with lots of undertow, so stay close to shore. There's also a lawn for picnicking and a children's playground. The

rocky nature of the bay also makes it ideal for lobster fishing, and colourful boats bob around on the water. Great local seafood such as fried swordfish or red snapper, lobster (in season), fish soup, pickled conch and shrimps, with delicious sides like cassava, sweet potato pie, rice and peas, green banana cou-cou, can be had at the local village rum shop/restaurant, **Bay Tavern** ① *T433 5118, daily 1000-1800*, which has picnic tables overlooking the bay, and on Thursday afternoon hosts a popular fish fry (or 'Thursday Lime') with DJ and music.

Bath

Around 7.5 km southeast of Bathsheba, with access off Highway 3, is the very pleasant beach and picnic spot at Bath. There are a few beach villas at one end, but otherwise this is an empty, unspoilt stretch with a long sweep of casuarina trees for shade. The sand is good but at high tide the sea covers it completely and you have to retreat into the trees. Low tide is wonderful with rock pools to wallow in for a lovely lazy day. Swimming is reasonably safe here because of an offshore reef,

> **Tip...**
>
> The 5-km hike between Bathsheba and Bath along the coastal paths – parts of which follow the old railway line (see box, page 66) – takes two to three hours. You can stop for lunch at Bay Tavern in Martin's Bay, the halfway point. This isn't an overly strenuous hike, and the few hills that need climbing aren't very steep or high.

but you have to be careful of the rocks. Popular with Barbadians at weekends, when families pitch camp around a picnic table, it is deserted during the week and highly recommended for escaping the crowds. Beach vendors sell cold drinks and tasty snacks, such as flying fish sandwiches, chips, chicken wings or fish cakes to fill a nagging hole, and facilities are good, with lifeguards, changing rooms with showers and toilets and plenty of parking. Not only is there a children's playground, there is also a large grass area for games such as football or cricket.

Codrington College

Sargeant St, St John, T416 8051, www.codrington.org. Daily 0900-1700. No entry fee but donations in the chapel appreciated.

Also in this area is Codrington College, one of the most famous landmarks on the island, which can be seen from the East Coast Road down an avenue of cabbage (Royal) palm trees. Built in 1743, it is the oldest Anglican theological college in the western hemisphere, and the solid and dignified main building was patterned after an Oxford college. It is steeped in history as the first Codrington landed in Barbados in 1628. His son acted as governor for three years but was dismissed for liberal views. Instead, he stood for parliament and was elected speaker for nine years. He was involved in several wars against the French and became probably the wealthiest man in the West Indies. The third Codrington succeeded his father as governor-general of the Leeward Islands, attempted to stamp out the considerable corruption of the time and distinguished himself in campaigns (especially in taking St Kitts). He died in 1710, a bachelor aged 42, and left his Barbadian properties to the Society for the Propagation of the Gospel in Foreign Parts. It was not until 1830 that Codrington College, where candidates could study for the Anglican priesthood, was established. From 1875 to 1955 it was associated with Durham University, England. Apart from its beautiful grounds and impressive façade, there is a chapel containing a plaque to Sir Christopher Codrington and a library.

Visitors are welcome to stroll around the gardens, where there is a beautiful lily pond (the flowers close up in the middle of the day) stocked with fish and ducks, and there are even picnic benches and a playground, with a wonderful view of the Atlantic coast behind the college. You can follow the track which drops down 120 m to the sea at the beautiful **Conset Bay**, where there is a tiny fishing village with an exceptionally long jetty where fishermen bringing in their catch.

Ragged Point

After Codrington College, another 7.5 km via Highway 3 and Highway 4 takes you to the most easterly point of Barbados, Ragged Point, from where (on a clear day) there is a spectacular view along almost the entire east coast of the island. The name conjures up images of desolation, jagged cliffs and rugged rocks, which is exactly what you will find here, and the East Point Lighthouse, also known as **Ragged Point Lighthouse**, perches on top of the 27-m cliffs. It was built in 1875 at a height of 29.5 m and, now automated, stands among the ruined houses of the former lighthouse keepers. An atmospheric station close to the shoreline measures air quality; this is the first landfall after blowing across the Atlantic from the coast of Africa. Experienced surfers might want to try out the surf at Ragged Point, but there are no easy routes down to the rocks; access to the waves is a descent down the cliff-face, which can be very slippery at the best of times. Remember to surf on the right-hand side of the bay as the left side is particularly treacherous.

South
coast

The south coast caters for the package holiday end of the market, with mid-range hotels packed in along the western end in districts with the charming English names of Hastings, Worthing and Dover, though there is little to distinguish them nowadays as the coast is entirely built up from Hastings to Oistins. The advantage of the south coast is that it is close to the airport and has better beaches with wider expanses of sand gently sloping down to the sea. It is popular with families and a younger crowd and there are plenty of restaurants, shops and bars; lively St Lawrence Gap, known as just The Gap, is the main district to go for nightlife, while Oistins, a fishing village, sparks into life on Friday nights for a fish fry. The south coast is great for all sorts of watersports, but watch out for rip tides if you are swimming.

The village of Six Cross Roads in the parish of St Philip is the main junction and point of reference in the southeast. From here Highway 5 heads towards Ragged Point and provides access to a number of beaches along this stretch of coast. In the southwest direction, Highway 5 goes from Six Cross Roads towards Oistins. There are also a couple of attractions within striking distance of the roundabout.

Sunbury Plantation House
St Philip, T423 6270, www.barbadosgreathouse.com. Daily 0900-1700, last entry 1630. US$10, children (5-12) US$5, under 5s free, restaurant in the courtyard. To get there, turn north on Highway 4B at Six Cross Roads roundabout, the plantation house is at the 1st T-junction.

One of the oldest houses on the island, Sunbury (pronounced Sun-berry) provides a fascinating insight into plantation life. It was built around 1660 from local rocks and ballast brought over in the ships from England and held together with a durable cement of limestone, sand, crushed coral and egg white. Originally it had a fishpond roof for collecting water but this was damaged in the 1780 hurricane and was replaced in 1788. The Chapman family who built the house were among the first settlers and were related to the Earl of Carlisle, who had granted them land. Chapmans are mentioned on Richard Ford's map of 1674, which shows a cattle mill on the Chapman plantation. It changed hands and names several times, owned by the Brankers, Butler Harris and the Barrow family (who named it Sunbury after their home in England). One of the Barrow heirs was Colonel in Charge during Bussa's (slave) Rebellion of 1816, during which the plantation suffered damage valued at £4000. The estate never really recovered and in 1835 John Barrow sold up and emigrated to Newfoundland.

The new owners, the Daniels, had made their money out of shipping sugar to England and owned several sugar estates, but they were absentee landlords. At the end of the 19th century, a Scotsman, Alistair Cameron, emigrated to Barbados, married a niece of the Barrows and in 1896 bought the Estates of Sunbury, Hampton and Bushy Park after the death of Thomas Daniel. Two of the Cameron daughters remained living at Sunbury until their deaths in 1980 and 1981, when the land was sold to the estate manager. The house, which had been untouched for 100 years, was bought by Angela and Keith Melville, who, in 1984, opened the whole of Sunbury Plantation House as a museum. But in 1995 a fire swept through the upper floors destroying the old timbers, wooden floors and antiques, except for those in the cellar; but the massive walls and a few floorboards were intact. A meticulous restoration was undertaken and the house reopened in 1996.

The house is now a museum and is crammed with a very busy collection of mahogany furniture, art, china and antiques. You can roam all over the house and in the cellars you can see the domestic quarters with a good collection of old optical instruments and household items. There are also numerous carts and gigs, including one donated by Sir Harry Llewellyn, the British Olympic showjumper of the 1950s and 1960s.

Foursquare Rum Distillery
Four Roads, St Philip, T248 9471. Mon-Fri 0900-1630. Free, tastings of 4 rums US$5. Buses stop in Four Roads; ask the driver to tell you when you get to Foursquare (it's fairly obvious when you see the old sugar chimney).

Approaching from Six Cross Roads roundabout along Highway 6 you will see the large compound of the Foursquare Rum Distillery to the left. This is the most modern rum distillery in Barbados and is set on 3 ha (8 acres) of a former sugar plantation and factory dating back to 1636. It produces several spiced rums including **Doorly's** and **Rum Sixty Six**. Visitors can follow the yellow footprints on the floor of the factory learning about the various stages of rum-making and seeing all the manufacturing processes, with the help of signage and photographs. There's an informative tasting session and the rums are available to buy at the **Copper Still Bar**.

★Bottom Bay

Beginning just south of Ragged Point, the string of beaches on the southeast coast starts at Bottom Bay, 7 km east of Six Cross Roads via Highway 5, and 800 m from the highway down a turning at Apple Hall (buses can drop at this junction). This has to be the most beautiful beach in Barbados and one of the best in the Caribbean. What is more, it is often deserted, even in high season, but even with a few couples on the beach you will feel as though you've got the place to yourselves. Steep cliffs surround the small bay and the sand is a glorious pale coral pink. You can park on the clifftop and then walk down steps carved between the cliffs onto a huge expanse of sand, where a clump of palm trees grows in true holiday brochure fashion. Sometimes there are boys on the beach who will offer to climb up to get coconuts down for you to drink the cool milk. There is a little hut under the coconut palms where you can usually hire sun loungers and umbrellas, but it is not always open mid-week or in low season. The only shade is under the palm trees or the cliffs, but with few other people around, that is usually plenty. The sea is often rough with quite big waves, better for jumping and splashing about than swimming. This area is becoming a popular part of the island to live in, and many new homes are being built on the clifftops. While there are no hotels in Bottom Bay, some places are available as holiday rentals. A short walk south along the cliff from Bottom Bay overlooking Cave Bay are the ruins of **Harrismith** plantation house that was built in 1920 and was once a hotel. You can park near this building; a long flight of stone steps carved into the cliff leads down to the beach. Also known as **Harrismith Beach**, Cave Bay has no facilities, and the strip of sand is narrower than that at Bottom Bay but palm trees grow behind the beach for shade and there is a lagoon formed by a reef, which gives protection for bathers.

Long Bay

The next beach to the west is on Long Bay, a glorious stretch of pink sand separated into three coves by cliffs with wooden steps going up from one beach and down to the next. Two of the bays front the former **Sam Lord's Castle Hotel Resort**, once the home of a notorious pirate who wrecked ships visiting the shores of the southeastern coast. Samuel Hall Lord (1778-1844) reputedly hung lanterns in the trees to look like the mouth of Carlisle Harbour and lure ships onto Cobbler's Reef where they were shipwrecked. There is said to be a tunnel from the beach to the castle's cellars. The

> **Tip...**
> The No 12A Transport Board bus from Fairchild Street Bus Terminal in Bridgetown follows the entire south and southeast coast via Hastings, Rockley Beach, Worthing, St Lawrence Gap, Maxwell, Oistins, Grantley Adams International Airport, Foul Bay, Crane Beach, Sam Lord's Castle, Long Bay, Apple Hall (for Bottom Bay) and ends in Merricks. Other buses do shorter sections of this route too: www.transportboard.com.

ON THE ROAD

The Gentleman Pirate

Stede Bonnet (1688-1718) was an unlikely Barbadian pirate because he was a wealthy landowner of a 400-acre estate southeast of Bridgetown. For some unexplained reason, and despite his lack of sailing experience, he abandoned his wife, children, land and fortune, and turned to piracy in 1717. It was rumoured he had marital problems, or he may have been having financial issues due to his sugarcane crop being wiped out by a hurricane or another natural disaster, or perhaps it was the worst midlife crisis of the 18th century. He bought a sloop with 10 guns, which was unusual as most pirates seized their ships by mutiny or converting a privateer vessel to a pirate ship. He named it *Revenge* and recruited a pirate crew of 70 and, in another break from tradition, paid his crew wages, not shares of plunder as most pirates did. Bonnet ran up the Jolly Roger and set off on the high seas, capturing other vessels in a series of colourful escapades along the Eastern Seaboard of what is now the United States. In Nassau, Bahamas, then known as the 'pirates' republic', he partnered with Edward Teach, better known as Blackbeard, the most famous and feared pirate of his day. Together they made several raids along the New England coast. Bonnet's downfall came when the governor of South Carolina commissioned Colonel William Rhett to capture him. In August 1718, Rhett cornered the *Revenge* at the mouth of the Cape Fear River and, after a violent firefight, managed to capture Bonnet and his crew. Bonnet tried to take advantage of his upper-class background by appealing to the governor for mercy and blaming everything on Blackbeard. But he was hanged on December 10, 1718, after less than two years of adventure, and just a month after Blackbeard had met his own bloody end in battle with the British Royal Navy. With his stylish clothes and powdered wig, Bonnet had stood out among the bearded, unkempt, ill-mannered pirates with whom he sailed and he was often referred to as the 'Gentleman Pirate'.

proceeds made him a wealthy man although the 'castle', a regency mansion built in 1820, was probably financed by his marriage to a wealthy heiress who later left him and fled to England. Another legend tells of how the captain of one of the wrecked ships murdered Sam Lord in London in 1844. In the 1970s, the castle was converted to a luxury hotel, attracting royalty and film stars, but it gradually declined until it was abandoned in 2003. Then in 2010 a mysterious fire gutted the once-magnificent building leaving only the shell. The brand new 450-room **Wyndham Grand Resort** ① www.wyndhamhotels.com, is currently under construction at the site and it is slated for completion in 2018. For now you can walk through the grounds and down steps to access the magnificent beach. Quiet and isolated with soft powdery sand, it makes an ideal spot for a picnic with plenty of shady trees, but there are no other facilities and beware of the sea as it's rough and unpredictable with strong undercurrents and rip tides.

Crane Beach

Crane Beach is another fabulously deep beach with plenty of powder soft coral pink sand and vibrant turquoise water. The waves are a bit rough for swimming but very popular with boogie-boarders and great for splashing about and generally having fun. Sun loungers, umbrellas and boogie boards can be hired on the beach and there are lifeguards. The **Crane Resort**, see page 85, is perched on top of cliffs at the southern end of the beach. It opened in 1887, making it the oldest continuously operating hotel on the island (although most of the resort buildings today are modern blocks and timeshare apartments). In the 18th century there was a crane on the top of the cliff for loading and unloading ships, hence the name. Sunday is a popular day at the resort, which puts on a breakfast accompanied by gospel and steel-pan music, followed by a huge Bajan buffet lunch at its **L'Azure**

Tip...
Just before the public beach access path, and bright yellow so hard to miss, is **Cutters Bajan Deli** (T423 0611, www.cutters.bb, Monday-Friday 0900-1700, Saturday and Sunday 0900-2000), which offers excellent fish cutters (sandwiches) plus other light meals and deli items to eat in or take away. Alternatively, you can pre-order a picnic or lunch which is delivered to you on the beach.

restaurant. You can even rent clothes so you can look decent when you come off the beach to eat in the restaurant, which has an eagle's eye view of the bay. The resort also has a shopping mall, **The Crane Village** – a reconstruction of a traditional Barbados town with a town hall, cobbled streets, gas lamps and wooden shuttered windows – where shops include a supermarket, an art gallery and a branch of Cave Shepherd for duty-free items. There's also the casual Italian **D'Onofrio's Trattoria** and **The Village Café**.

If you park at the resort they will charge you access through their grounds (with a glass elevator or steps down to the beach), redeemable against a drink at the bar or meal at one of the restaurants. Alternatively, carry on to a little roundabout and turn down a narrow lane which leads to a car park where stepping stones give access to the southern end of the beach.

Foul Bay

Just south of Crane Beach, on the other side of the roundabout, is Foul Bay; if driving, take the turning signed 'Public Access to Foul Bay Beach' which will take you down Foul Bay Road to a car park. This is another long stretch of idyllic pink sand with turquoise water, wide and open and less crowded than Crane, although conditions in the sea are similar. It is the longest beach on this part of the coast, with large cliffs at each end. There are toilets and showers, some shade under casuarina and palm trees and a few picnic tables and benches, so it's ideal if you want to be self-sufficient and take your own picnic. A small fishing fleet comes ashore here and you can sometimes see turtles just beyond the waves.

Fact...
Foul Bay is in fact a corruption of the original name, Fowl Bay, which originated from the large number of migrating birds that once nested in the area.

Barbados Concorde Experience

Grantley Adams International Airport, Christ Church, T420 7738, www.barbadosconcorde.com. Tue-Sat 0900-1700. US$20, children (2-12) US$12.50, under 2s free.

Grantley Adams International Airport is located in Seawell, Christ Church, 6 km south of Six Cross Roads, 16 km east of Bridgetown and easily accessible off Tom Adams Highway. An odd place for a tourist attraction, but the Barbados Concorde Experience is in a hangar at the airport and is definitely worthwhile. In 1976, the supersonic British/French-built, turbojet-powered, passenger jet airliner, Concorde, began transatlantic flights between London and Paris and New York in half the time of regular aircraft. Only 20 planes were ever built and the fleet was retired in 2003. Seven of these aircraft are now housed in museums around the world – four in the UK, two in the US and one in Barbados. Concorde first came to Barbados in 1977 to take Queen Elizabeth II back to the UK after a royal visit in her Jubilee year. It again transported the Queen and her party to/from the island in 1987 and 2003, and flew between London and Barbados during the winter holiday season between 1984 and 1991 (by then it was fully owned by British Airways). At the Concorde Experience, guides will escort you on to the impressive plane to walk along the aisle between the rows of seats and peek in the cockpit (behind a glass wall) and explain all the features and capabilities of Concorde.

Additionally, there are information panels about the history of flight technology in general, and the history of aviation in Barbados (the first plane came to the island in 1913, the first passenger service started in 1939 and the first airport terminal was built in 1942). An excellent sound and light show projects vintage Concorde footage on to the side of the plane.

Tip...
The hangar housing Concorde G-BOAE is just three minutes' walk from the check-in desks of Grantley Adams International Airport. Check in early; it takes about one hour to visit and there are facilities for storing bulky hand luggage.

The southwest coast

the main beach resort area with hotels and apartments lining the coast

The southwest coast is a string of beautiful expanses of white sandy beaches backed by hotels, bars and restaurants, within striking distance of Grantley Adams International Airport and where public transport is readily available. It's not as glitzy as the west coast, nor is it as expensive, but it is popular with package holidaymakers and has all the facilities they may need for some fun in the sun.

Enterprise (Miami) Beach

Off Highway 7 just east of Oistins, is the 230-m-long Enterprise Beach, also known as Miami Beach. This good and popular beach is in two parts: the western side offers calm waters and is ideal for children to wade and swim, while the eastern side has occasional swells and adds a little more excitement to swimming. You should, however, avoid the water near the cliffs at the end, especially at high tide, and the general rule everywhere is to stay within your depth. There is a lifeguard station between the two bays. Lots of Barbadians come here, especially at the weekends, and early morning or before sunset for a stroll, jog or dip in the sea. There's plenty of shade under casuarina and broadleaf trees and everything you could need for a pleasant day on the beach, including sun lounger and umbrella rental, toilets, picnic tables and the Mr Delicious Snack Bar ⓘ *daily 1000-1800*, which is an old bus that offers excellent fish cutters, rum punch and lemonade. Catamaran tour parties often anchor here for lunch and windsurfing is popular, particularly for those at an intermediate level.

From Enterprise Beach there is a good view of **South Point Lighthouse**, the oldest lighthouse

Tip...
Many buses travel from Bridgetown along Highway 7 south coast route to Oistins and beyond; get off at the Oistins Post Office stop and follow the pathway from there about 250 m to Enterprise Beach.

ON THE ROAD

★ Oistins Fish Fry

Held at Bay Gardens near the fish market, Oistins Fish Fry is a major street party on a Friday night for both Barbadians and tourists. Bus loads of tourists are ferried in from resorts around the island and it's a lot of fun. Excellent flying fish, as well as tuna, swordfish, barracuda, kingfish, marlin, mahi mahi and lobster, with sides of coleslaw, green salad, baked macaroni pie, rice and peas and hot sauce, are all served in an extremely informal setting from about 30 or so wooden stalls. It attracts hundreds of hungry people keen to fill up before hitting the bars and night spots of the south coast and food is usually available from around 1800. There's also plenty of drinking too, karaoke, steelpan bands, and live calypso and reggae on the main stage area for dancing. For a big plateful of food, expect to pay in the region of US$15, and about US$3 for a bottle of Banks beer and US$6 for a rum punch. A smaller event happens on Saturday night, and on other nights many stalls do food and some bars are open, but it is low key and mostly caters for locals liming and playing dominoes.

in Barbados, which was reassembled on the southernmost point of the island in 1852, one year after being shown at London's Great Exhibition. At 27 m high and painted with thick horizontal lines of red and white, the grounds (but not the tower) are open to the public; follow the signs through the residential area of **Atlantic Shores**, just to the east of Enterprise Beach.

Oistins

Oistins, the main town in the parish of Christ Church, is 8 km west of Grantley Adams International Airport. It was named after plantation owner Edward Oistin. After the execution of King Charles I in 1649, Barbados declined to acknowledge Oliver Cromwell and his commonwealth parliament. This resulted in six months of resistance to Cromwell's fleet in 1651, which led to the signing of the 'Articles of Agreement' in a tavern called the 'Ye Mermaid's Inn' in Oistins on 11 January 1652. This was later acknowledged as the Charter of Barbados by the Parliament in England. Oistins Beach is divided into two bays, separated by rocks and the jetty. It is now the main fishing port on the south coast, with colourful boats pulled up on the shore. The Oistins Fish Market is worth visiting, even if you don't want to buy, to see the expert skill and lightning speed with which the women fillet flying fish and bag them up for sale. Oistins is also the venue for an **Easter Fish Festival**, see page 14, celebrating fishermen's skills with demonstrations of fish boning, boat racing and crab racing, helped along with steel pan music and dancing.

The **Christ Church Parish Church** ① *Church Hill Rd, T428 8087, www.anglican. bb/~christchurch, Mon-Fri 0930-1700, Sun services 0600, 0745, 0915*, overlooks the town (a bit of a steep walk up) and is the fifth parish church to be built on the site. The original was constructed in 1629 and that and subsequent structures were all destroyed by natural disasters including flood, fire and hurricanes. The present Anglican church was built in 1935 and has an impressive barrel-vaulted ceiling, a fine stained-glass altar window and is flanked by a large, wooded graveyard which is notable for containing the Chase Vault. When the vault was opened in 1812 for the burial of Colonel Thomas Chase, the lead coffins were mysteriously found scattered around inside. It happened again in 1816, 1817, 1819 and 1820, whereupon the coffins were removed and buried separately in the churchyard. Whatever had been moving them around had thrown them about with such violence that the wooden coffin of Mrs Thomasina Goddard (1807) had smashed to splinters and taken a chunk out of the vault wall. To this day no conclusive explanation has been given for this bizarre occurrence.

Welches Beach and Maxwell Beach
West from Oistins, Highway 7 runs right along the edge of Welches Beach, which was once a tiny bay with little or no shoreline, but has recently been redeveloped and, by adding more sand, is now quite wide with a nicely landscaped boardwalk. However, there are few facilities here; no sun lounger and umbrella rental or lifeguards on duty, so swim with caution as the sea can be rough at times with some undertow.

Highway 7 veers inland slightly and a turn-off for about 350 m down Maxwell Coast Road (ask buses to drop you here) takes you to Maxwell Beach. It has lovely coral-white sand and the water is fairly calm, even for supervised small children. There are several hotels in the Maxwell area so the beach can get busy, but there is still plenty of space. Several watersports can be arranged including banana boat and inflatable doughnut rides, Hobie cats and jet skiing. You can rent sun loungers and umbrellas and the woodland area adjacent to the car park has picnic tables under shady trees and there are toilets.

Dover Beach and St Lawrence Gap
Between Maxwell and the southern end of the popular tourist area of St Lawrence Gap, Dover Beach is a beautiful horseshoe-shaped bay lined with hotels and with pristine white sand and turquoise water; picture-postcard stuff. It's a great place for lazing around, sun-bathing and cooling off in the sea, which is usually calm and protected and there's a lifeguard station. On the beachfront is a timber boardwalk, with numerous stalls selling everything from drinks, ice creams and snacks to suntan lotion, hats, T-shirts, beachwear and snorkelling gear. Picnic tables are scattered around the beach, sun loungers and umbrellas can be rented, and kayaks, Hobie cats, boogie boards, windsurfers and jet skis are avalable.

'The Gap', as St Lawrence Gap is usually called, begins at Dover Beach and runs westwards along a 1.5-km stretch of coast road that runs parallel to Highway 7 as far as Worthing. The beach below the 'gap', or road, is quite rocky and there's not much sand, but there's a wooden boardwalk with benches and the sea here is mostly calm and shallow at low tide and is good for a paddle. St Lawrence Gap is the main nightlife strip in Barbados with many restaurants, bars and clubs, some of which are in idyllic locations overlooking the water. The larger resorts are at the eastern end of Dover Beach (including the vast all-inclusive, adults-only Sandals Barbados), while the bars and restaurants, souvenir shops, fast-food outlets and apartment blocks are mostly towards the western end of The Gap. Near the **Southern Palms Hotel**, there's another **Chattel House Shopping Village** (the other is at Holetown, see page 49), which has several kiosks, replicas of traditional brightly painted wooden chattel houses, that sell souvenirs and gifts. Dover Beach and The Gap are unashamedly touristy, but the atmosphere is always lively with everybody in a holiday mood.

Perched on a small cliff at the first corner you come to as you enter The Gap from Worthing is the photogenic **St Lawrence Anglican Church** ① *T420 7679, www.anglican. bb/stlawrence, daily 0900-1700*, which dates from 1838 and is probably the oldest, most traditional building located along The Gap.

Worthing Beach

Just after the church, St Lawrence Gap's lively street turns northwards and joins Highway 7 at Worthing and the string of resorts, apartments, bars and restaurants continues further along the coast past Worthing Beach, also known (rather unimaginatively) as **Sandy Beach**. The curve of the coastline and an offshore reef has produced a lovely beach with pure white sand and clear, calm, shallow water, almost in a lagoon, making it ideal for families with small children; you may even see turtles. Beach vendors rent out sun loungers, umbrellas and watersports equipment. At the southeastern end of the beach (south of **Coral Sands Beach Resort**) there are two beach bars close to each other worth seeking out for an enjoyable afternoon. **Crystal Waters Beach Bar** ① *T435 6532, daily 1100-2000*, serves great bar snacks including ham cutters and fish cakes and more substantial meals like blackened fish and macaroni pie, and on Sunday there's a very popular barbecue (phone ahead to make a reservation); food is served 1230-1430 and then there's live music and a party until 1900. Close by is **Coast Beach Café & Lounge** ① *T622 1858, www.coastbarbados.com, daily 1000-2300*, which offers Caribbean and Italian food and another Sunday party with a DJ (1900-0200).

Rockley (Accra) Beach

The next beach west along Highway 7, Rockley Beach is a family-friendly, 300-m curl of white sand. It is often referred to as Accra Beach after the all-inclusive **Accra Beach Hotel & Spa** that dominates it. Again it's quite lovely but still in the middle of the hotel strip so is understandably popular and often crowded. There are lifeguards, a changing facility with toilets and showers and a car park; sun loungers and umbrellas can be hired. The many buses that ply the main south coast route stop close to the beach. Behind the sand wooden stalls selling food and drink and Barbadian crafts in the shade of casuarina and sea grape trees. The southeastern end of the beach is perfect for smaller children as there is a pool-like area protected by rocks that break the force of the waves and where the water stays shallow for a long way out. At the northwestern end, watersports vendors rent out boogie boards, Hobie cats and windsurfers on the rougher waves. Strong swimmers can head out to a 100-m-long man-made reef of huge boulders for some snorkelling. The reef was sunk in the late 1990s and is now home to coral and large schools of blue tang, jacks and other colourful fish; there's a possibility of seeing hawksbill turtles. It's marked at each end by two large posts protruding from the water and is surrounded by a sandy seabed, but as the waves can break on top of the rock dump, visibility can be poor at times. You must be careful on such a young reef not to damage anything by standing on it or poking around with your hands; coral dies if you touch it.

The two standout beach bars at Rockley (Accra) Beach are: **Oasis Beach Bar** ① *T239-3410, Mon-Fri 0900-1700, Sat-Sun 1000-1800*, a kiosk in front of the **Accra Beach Hotel & Spa** famous for its combination of rum punch and Bajan fish cakes; and **The Tiki Bar** ① *T435 8074, www.tikibarbados.com, daily 0900-2300*, which has a broad wooden deck at the southeastern end of the beach and offers a good menu, more than 60 cocktails, free sun loungers and showers for patrons, as well as live music on Friday and Saturday evenings. Behind the beach and across Highway 7, **Quayside Centre Shopping Plaza** is a small strip mall with beachwear, souvenir and gift shops, a well-stocked supermarket, and a few places to eat including an ice cream parlour and a coffee shop. Just north of the Quayside Centre Shopping Plaza (and not surprisingly on Golf Club Road) is the **Rockley Golf & Country Club** (see page 96).

Hastings

The wide, wooden South Coast Boardwalk (officially renamed the Sir Richard Haynes Boardwalk in 2012 after the late Barbadian politician) starts at Rockley (Accra) Beach's western end and zig-zags along the shore to just west of the SoCo Hotel in Hastings; about 1.5 km. It makes a pleasant stroll or a good early morning jog and a few tiny sandy coves allow you to step down on to the sand for sunbathing or a paddle, although you might need to watch out for crabs. There are a number of bars and restaurants along the route and places to sit and watch the world go by. Police patrol the boardwalk at night, but take care if walking as it is mostly unlit.

Hastings village dates from 1836 and was one of Barbados' first tourist resorts when residents of Bridgetown came by carriage to visit the Hastings Rocks to enjoy the fresh sea breeze. Along the seafront were wooden bathhouses standing in the shallow waters on stilts; bathers would get changed and then descend the stairs into the ocean to swim. Hotels were established in the Hastings area as early as 1887. Today it's practically a suburb of Bridgetown, and where the boardwalk ends, you are on Hastings Main Road (part of Highway 7), which then runs only another kilometre or so westwards to the Garrison Savannah and St Anne's Fort. Hastings has a beautiful white sandy beach dotted with palm trees where turtles are routinely spotted in its crystal-clear waters. With a gently sloping sea shelf, it's safe for children to paddle in – just avoid the rocky sections of the beach; moderate waves and undertow means caution is advised when swimming far out. There are no sun loungers/umbrellas to hire or any other facilities, but plenty of cafés and fast-food outlets are on Hastings Main Road or back on the boardwalk. Additionally, **Lanterns at Hastings** ⓘ *Hastings Main Rd, Christ Church, T271 0069, www.lanternsmall. com, daily 0900-2100*, is a modern two-storey mall with 30 shops and restaurants and a large car park.

An unusual attraction in Hastings is the **Mallalieu Motor Collection** ⓘ *Pavilion Court, Hastings Main Rd (Highway 7), T426 4640, US$10, Mon-Fri 0900-1530, Sat-Sun by appointment.* It is one man's lifetime collection of more than 20 vintage cars crammed into a large garage. The number one vehicle in Bill Mallalieu's line-up is a Bentley made for Prince Bernhard of The Netherlands in 1947 and raced in the 1949 Monte Carlo Rally. There's also a Daimler, Humber, Vanden Plas Princess, Wolseley, Lanchester and many others. Every car has a story to tell and Bill is a great raconteur; he is usually there in the mornings. The walls of the garage are also covered with photographs – the island's first bus, police car, taxi, etc, with pieces of information pinned up alongside. It's an interesting way to spend an hour or so if you like old cars, especially British ones.

Listings Barbados

Tourist information

Barbados National Trust
Wildey House, Wildey, St Michael, T426 2421, www.barbadosnationaltrust.org, see also Facebook. Mon-Fri 0830-1630.
The headquarters of the Barbados National Trust, Wildey House, is a beautiful old Georgian mansion set in 2 ha (5 acres) of grounds and woods. The house and its contents were bequeathed to the Trust by Edna Leacock, and if you visit, ask for a tour of the main public rooms to see fine collections of Victorian china, crystal, books and mahogany furniture. The Trust can give you details/schedules for the **Open House Programme** (see box, page 18) and the Sun hikes they organize (see page 96).

Barbados Tourism Marketing Inc (BTMI)
1st floor, Warrens Office Complex, off ABC Highway near Massy Stores Supermarket, Warrens, T535 3700, www.visitbarbados.org. Mon-Fri 0830-1630.
This is the main office for what was previously the Barbados Tourism Authority, and now is primarily involved in the promotion of Barbados as a tourist destination; they also maintain offices in New York, Miami, Canada, the UK and Germany. They are a little way out of the centre of Bridgetown, but nevertheless are very helpful if you drop by and the website is a good source of information. There is also an office at the **Bridgetown Cruise Terminal** at the Deep Water Harbour, T426 1718, daily 0900-1700 when cruise ships are in port. Contact details for BTMI offices abroad can be found on the website.

Ins and Outs of Barbados is a glossy, annual publication with lots of historical articles as well as advertising and a useful year-round calendar. Similar publications include *Barbados in a Nutshell* and *Visit Barbados*. All 3 can be picked up in hotels, are available as e-guides or can be downloaded as PDFs from **Miller Publishing Company** (www.millerpublishing.net).

Good free maps published by the tourism associations can also be found at reception desks of hotels and car hire companies will provide them.

Where to stay

Unless otherwise stated, all hotel rooms have a/c, TV and Wi-Fi. Hotel VAT (7.5%) and service charge (10%) is charged across the board, usually as a single charge of 17.5%. Check if this has been included in quoted rates.

Bridgetown *maps pages 32 and 50.*
There isn't much need to stay in Bridgetown itself when the nicer beaches are so tantalizingly close. There are some all-inclusive resorts south of the centre off Bay St in Carlisle Bay: **Island Inn Hotel** (www.islandinnbarbados.com) and the **Radisson Aquatica Resort Barbados** (www.radisson.com) are just to the south of the Barbados Yacht Club, and the **Hilton Barbados Resort** is at Needham's Point (www.hiltonbarbados resort.com). Only 1 km or so beyond or east of the Garrison Historic Area on Highway 7 you're in Hastings, the start of a long line of resorts and apartments that goes all the way along the south coast (see box, page 82).

$$$ Sweetfield Manor
Brittons New Rd, Brittons Hill, Bridgetown, St Michael, T429 8356, www.sweetfield manor.com.
An early 1900s white-painted, shuttered wooden plantation home on a hilltop in the eastern suburbs of Bridgetown, and now an atmospheric, upmarket, antique-filled B&B with lawns, a kitchen garden, koi fish pond, swimming pool and 10 rooms, either in the main house, courtyard or garden. Elegant and relaxing, the excellent breakfasts run to

everal courses, but a car is useful to get to restaurants, beaches and attractions.

$$ Nautilus Beach Apartments
Bay St, Bridgetown, St Michael, T426 3541, www.nautilusbeachapartments.com.
Nothing fancy but if you want somewhere cheap close to the centre of Bridgetown (a 15-min walk), these 15 no-frills apartments in a blue-and-white block will do for a night. Dated furnishings but clean with tiled floors and kitchenettes, some have patios or balconies, a/c or fans, close to Brownes Beach and the Garrison Historic Area.

West coast *map page 50.*
The Platinum Coast is so named for its very expensive accommodation, but good-quality cheaper self-catering accommodation can also be found if you are prepared to walk a few mins to the beach; check out the rental agencies on page 23 or try **Airbnb**.

$$$$ Cobblers Cove
Road View, 1 km south of Speightstown, St Peter, T422 2291, www.cobblerscove.com.
Based around the Great House built in 1943 as a seaside mansion by a plantation owner, this has 40 ultra-chic suites in the beautiful bird-filled gardens. The beach is narrow but there's a pool, plus an elegant sea-view restaurant (with dress code), a spa, watersports, tennis, and a gym that offers yoga and pilates. A member of **Relais & Chateaux** with excellent service and a high proportion of repeat well-heeled British clientele. B&B or all-inclusive.

$$$$ The Colony Club by Elegant Hotels
Folkestone, St James, T422 2335, www.eleganthotels.com/colony-club.
A 10-min walk to Holetown, this family-friendly faux-colonial-style low-rise property is popular with British holidaymakers and spreads over mature grounds with soaring palms and mahogany trees and 4 swimming pools. 96 smart rooms with terraces/balconies, large open-air restaurant, swim-up pool bar,

and free water taxi to/from the 2 other Elegant Hotels on the west coast. Rates are B&B and include non-motorized watersports.

$$$$ Coral Reef Club
Porters, 1.6 km north of Holetown, St James, T422 2372, www.coralreefbarbados.com.
Run by the O'Hara family since the 1950s and spread over 5 ha (12 acres) of glorious gardens with paths, ponds and lawns running down to the sea, this delivers graceful, old-school luxury in 88 plantation-style cottages and villas with wooden balustrading, fretwork and shuttered windows. Elegant dining with evening entertainment, complimentary tennis clinic most evenings, spa, and large swimming pool with columns and terrace. B&B or half board.

$$$$ The House by Elegant Hotels
Paynes Bay, St James, T432 5525, www.eleganthotels.com/the-house.
An adults-only property with 34 suites around a courtyard, modern stylish interiors and well regarded for its service and atmosphere – the staff 'ambassadors' tend to your every need from a jet-lag revival massage to providing ice cream and cold flannels while you tan. Not quite an all-inclusive like the other Elegant Hotels properties; rates include champagne breakfast, afternoon tea and evening canapés, but not dinner – eat at the on-site **Daphne's** restaurant which offers modern Italian cuisine (open to all) or elsewhere on the Platinum Coast.

$$$$ Little Good Harbour
Shermans, 3 km north of Speightstown, St Lucy, T439 3000, www.littlegood harbourbarbados.com.
Low-key, relaxed and out-of-the-way, offering 19 attractive wooden cottages with kitchens, some are double-storey with 2-3 bedrooms, set in pretty gardens around 2 pools across the road from the sea, with spa, gym and free kayaks. Rates are room-only. **The Fish Pot** restaurant is excellent

All-inclusive options on Barbados

There are numerous all-inclusive resorts on Barbados, most of which sit on beautiful beaches and have one or more swimming pools and watersports. Most packages provide three meals a day, an afternoon snack, appetizers at cocktail hour, and non-alcoholic and house drinks. Breakfast and lunch are normally buffets, while the evening meal might be a themed buffet, a barbecue, or a set menu with three or four choices; the larger resorts can have several restaurants and bars. They vary in price considerably; at the cheaper end they might be sprawling properties featuring blocky-style rooms and mediocre meals, while at the top end, there are intimate luxury hideaways with stylish interiors and gourmet food. The downsides of staying at an all-inclusive are: unless you eat and drink a lot, their value is not always any greater than paying for meals as you go; some of them can be rather soulless places where you will only mix with guests of one nationality (depending on where the resort is marketed), many of whom may not even leave the property for their entire holiday; the food may start to look and taste similar after a few days; and any extras (boat trips, spa treatments and the like) will be very expensive. But on the plus side, you know exactly what you are getting for your money (especially if you combine flights and transfers in a package) and service, facilities and location are generally very good. If all-inclusive does appeal, here are some examples:

Accra Beach Hotel & Spa, Rockley (Accra) Beach, Christ Church, www.accrabeachhotel.com.
Almond Beach Resort, Heywoods Beach, St Peter, www.almondbarbados.com.
Barbados Beach Club, Maxwell Beach, Christ Church, www.barbadosbeach club.com.
The Club, Barbados Resort & Spa, Holetown, St James, www.theclubbarbados.com.
Crystal Cove by Elegant Hotels, Appleby, St James, www.eleganthotels.com.
Discovery Bay by Rex Resorts, Holetown, St James, www.rexresorts.com.
Island Inn Hotel, Carlisle Bay, Bridgetown, St Michael, www.islandinnbarbados.com.
Mango Bay Barbados, Holetown, St James, www.mangobaybarbados.com.
Radisson Aquatica Resort Barbados, Carlisle Bay, Bridgetown, St Michael, www.radisson.com.
Sandals Barbados, Dover Beach, Christ Church, www.sandals.com.
Savannah Beach Hotel, Hastings, Christ Church, T434 3800, www.savannahbarbados.com.
Sea Breeze Beach Hotel, Maxwell Beach, Christ Church, www.sea-breeze.com.
The SoCo Hotel, Hastings, Christ Church, www.thesocohotel.com.
Sugar Bay Barbados, Hastings, Christ Church, www.sugarbaybarbados.com.
Turtle Beach by Elegant Hotels, Dover Beach, Christ Church, www.eleganthotels.com.
Waves Hotel & Spa by Elegant Hotels, Prospect Bay, St James, www.eleganthotels.com.

(open to all, see page 89) and is on the ocean-side of the coastal road. Sister hotel to the east-coast **Atlantis Hotel** (see page 84).

$$$$ Lone Star
Mount Standfast, 3 km north of Holetown, St James, T419 0599, www.thelonestar.com.

Boutique hotel with just 4 huge suites and 2 villas with beachfront terraces, stylishly decorated with 4-poster beds and billowing white fabrics. The building was originally a garage built in the 1940s by Romy Reid who ran a bus company and called himself the Lone Star of the west coast; later it was a nightclub and then a house, owned by Mrs Robertson of the jam company who water-skied offshore until her late 80s. The highly regarded restaurant sits right on the beach (see page 88) and meal plans are available.

$$$$ The Sandpiper
Holetown, St James, T422 2372, www.sandpiperbarbados.com.
Smaller and more informal than the sister property **Coral Reef Club** (see above), but still luxurious and spread around tropical gardens, 50 rooms and suites, some with kitchenette, 2 swimming pools, a romantic open-air restaurant fringed by koi-filled ponds, inviting beach bar, gym and 2 tennis courts. Guests can use the spa at Coral Reef Club, a 10-min drive away (free transfers provided). B&B or half board.

$$$$-$$$ Bayfield House
Crescent Dr, Mullins, St Peter, T419 049, www.bayfieldbarbados.com.
Impeccably run by Trevor and Pamela Ramsay, this 1930s plantation-style guesthouse is up a quiet side lane about a 5-min walk to Mullins Beach. It sits in an expansive garden with a cannon on the front lawn and an attractive oval swimming pool. The 10 rooms share the large wraparound verandas furnished with rocking chairs and fern-filled pots. Rates include a good breakfast, and dinners are offered a couple of nights a week. No TVs or children under 12.

$$$$-$$$ Tamarind by Elegant Hotels
Paynes Bay, St James, T432 1332, www.eleganthotels.com/tamarind.
Another Elegant Hotels quality property in a prime location towards the southern end of Paynes Bay, very comfortable with 104 large rooms and suites on 3 floors overlooking pleasant gardens leading on to the beach, where there are plenty of watersports. Indoor or outdoor dining available. Rates are all-inclusive, half-board or full-board and guests get credits for meals/drinks at the 3 other Elegant Hotels sister properties on the west coast (reached by water taxi).

$$$ Beach View Barbados
Paynes Bay, St James, T432 2300, www.beachviewbarbados.com.
On the inland side of Highway 1 and a short walk from the beach at Paynes Bay (though you need to cross the busy coastal road), modern and fresh looking with neat lawns and floral walkways, the 36 1- to 3-bedroom apartments (with dishwasher, washing machine and dryer) are popular with families and occupy 3- and 4-storey buildings that form a U-shape around a pool area. Rates are room-only, a café is open 0800-1400 for breakfast and lunch, and there's a rooftop bar and other restaurants close by.

$$$ Sugar Cane Club Hotel & Spa
Maynards, St Peter, T422 5026, www.sugarcaneclub.com.
An inland option set in peaceful grounds with tiered lawns dotted with sun loungers (you can often see green monkeys). The 44 spacious rooms are in 2- and 3-storey Mediterranean-style whitewashed and terracotta-roofed buildings with kitchenettes and patios/balconies. Facilities include 2 pools, spa, gym, squash court, mountain bikes, 2 bars and a smart, airy restaurant. Free daytime shuttles to Heywoods Beach (2 km) and Speightstown (3 km). Room-only or all-inclusive, no children under 14.

$$$ Tropical Sunset Beach Apartment Hotel
West Haven Complex, Holetown, St James, T432 2715, www.tropicalsunsetbarbados.com.
From US$175 per night room-only in low season, this 4-storey modern block is one of the least inexpensive places on the west coast – and it's right on the beach. 23 simple

but adequate rooms with kitchenettes and balcony, can sleep a family of 4, small pool and sun loungers on the beach, very convenient with lots of restaurants close by and a shopping centre across the road.

$$ Legend Garden Condos
Highway 1B, Mullins, St Peter, T422 8369, www.legendcondos.com.

Run by Canadian Delia and her Barbadian husband Bird, Legend Garden Condos are up an extended driveway across the road from Mullins Beach, comprising 8 1-bed and 1 2-bed apartments with good kitchenettes, no a/c but ceiling fans, and set in quiet tropical gardens with a pool and patios and the odd green monkey. Decor is a little frilly but apartments are spacious and, at US$150 in high season, are exceptionally good value for the west coast. No breakfast but restaurants and supermarket close by.

$$ Villa Marie Guesthouse
Lashley Rd, Fitts Village, St James, T417 5799, www.barbados.org/villas/villamarie.

This quiet guesthouse, up a side road, is run by Peter (German) and has 3 large rooms, 2 apartments (sleeping 4) with kitchen, a huge communal kitchen and dining room, pleasant garden with mature trees, sun loungers and barbecue. Breakfast is not provided but it's 5 mins' walk from a supermarket, 200 m from the beach and bus stop on the main road. Doubles from US$95, a/c an extra US$10, and the whole house can be rented for groups.

East coast *map page 50.*

$$$ Atlantis Hotel
Tent Bay, Bathsheba, St Joseph, T433 9445, www.atlantishotelbarbados.com.

A 10-min walk to Bathsheba Beach, in a spectacular setting on the water's edge with waves crashing below, this hotel opened in 1884 alongside the railway line and became a much-loved institution under the management of Enid Maxwell who ran it from 1945-2001. Now owned by Australian

Andrew Warden, who also owns **Little Good Harbour** on the west coast, it has 8 rooms and 2 apartments, is elegant and understated with whitewashed tongue-and-groove panelling, louvered shutters, muslin-swathed beds and polished pine floorboards. B&B, good restaurant, popular with day-tippers, especially for the buffet lunches (see page 89).

$$$ Sea-U Guest House
Tent Bay, Bathsheba, St Joseph, T433 9450, www.seaubarbados.com.

Quiet and peaceful with rustic charm and run by Uschi (German). It's a 10-min walk to Bathsheba Beach and a 5-min walk uphill to Andromeda Botanic Gardens. 9 rooms in 2 wooden houses with whitewashed walls and shutters, most have kitchenettes, although not all have a/c (sea breezes suffice), with hammocks on the balconies and between palm trees on the lawns. Ample buffet breakfast served in a gazebo alongside the main house; 3-course set menu dinner US$30.

$$ Round House Inn
Bathsheba, St Joseph, T433 9678, www.roundhousebarbados.com.

This building dates from 1832 and overlooks the sea from the hillside. There are 4 rooms in the domed round part, all different, one, considerably nicer than the others, has a roof terrace, while the others are cramped but light and bright with details such as original skylights, deep-set windows, and original staircases that give it some charm. B&B, good restaurant, the best place to eat in the evenings in Bathsheba and is open to all, with a lovely terrace perched above Bathsheba Beach and overlooking the famous Soup Bowl.

South coast *map page 50.*

Most of the south coast is wall-to-wall hotels from Hastings to Dover popular with package holidaymakers. It's close to the airport, with plenty of watersports and nightlife.

$$$ The Crane
Crane, St Philip, T423 6220,
www.thecrane.com.
The Crane first opened its doors in 1887 and is in a spectacular clifftop setting, but the extra blocky timeshare units have totally changed its character. There's a glass elevator down to the pink-sand Crane Beach, plus 5 swimming pools, including an impressive 6000-sq-m (1½-acre) cascading complex, 2 floodlit tennis courts, 4 restaurants, a spa, gym and the Crane Village shopping mall. 252 rooms and 1- and 2-bed apartments with kitchens, all spacious and modern with patios/balconies, although only 18 luxury rooms are in the old hotel and these have vaulted ceilings and 4-poster beds. B&B.

$$$$-$$$ Little Arches Boutique Hotel
Enterprise Beach Rd, Christ Church, T420 4689,
www.littlearches.com.
This super-friendly, vibrant salmon-pink, hacienda-style adults-only hotel is 150 m from Enterprise (Miami) Beach and has quirky colourful touches such as mosaic tiles, chandeliers and a triangular-shaped swimming pool. The excellent restaurant, **Café Luna** (see page 90) is on the rooftop with sea views. The 10 rooms have terracotta floors, 4-poster beds and attractive bathrooms but vary a lot in size and price – the cheaper rooms don't have a private terrace, while the more expensive ones have their own plunge pool. Rates are room-only.

$$$$-$$ Butterfly Beach Hotel
Maxwell Main Rd (highway 7), Oistins, Christ Church T428 9095, www.butterflybeach.com.
This low-key beachfront hotel has the **Reef Bar and Grill** restaurant and 93 units: rooms, studios, 1- and 2-bed apartments with kitchenettes and either floor-to-ceiling windows or balconies – rates vary from US$100 for a room with no view in low season to US$$325 for an ocean-view 2-bed apartment in high season. There's only a strip of narrow sand here but it has a pool with sundeck, there's a bus stop outside to get to other beaches and **Oistins Fish Fry** is within walking distance. Breakfast US$12.

$$$ Bougainvillea Beach Resort
Maxwell Coast Rd, Christ Church, T418 0990,
www.bougainvillearesort.com.
Right on Maxwell Beach, this family-friendly resort has 138 bright and spacious rooms in several cream and pink 4-storey blocks, all with kitchens. Some rooms sleep 4. Facilities include 3 swimming pools, 2 attractive open-air restaurants, kids' club, and free use of boogie boards, kayaks and snorkelling gear. Room-only or all-inclusive.

$$$ Coral Sands Beach Resort
Worthing Beach, T435 6617,
www.coralsandsresort.com.
Comfortable and affordable family resort with 31 large sea-view studios with kitchenettes, large balconies, tiled floors, floral bedspreads and curtains and white wicker furniture in a single 4-storey building. There's a decent bar by the smallish pool but the dining room is characterless and breakfast is rather overpriced (rates are room-only). It's better to self-cater (a good supermarket is nearby) and it's only a 5-min walk to restaurants and nightlife at The Gap.

$$$ Magic Isle Beach Apartments
Rockley Beach, Christ Church, T435 6760,
www.magicislebarbados.com.
Simple and slightly old-fashioned but clean and well maintained, 30 sea-facing apartments sleeping up to 4 in 4-storey blocks, a gate at the bottom of the garden dotted with a few palms and a good-sized pool leads directly on to one end of Rockley (Accra) Beach and the boardwalk, and there is a supermarket as well as a number of affordable places to eat and drink close by.

$$$ Ocean Two
Dover Beach, Christ Church, T418 1800,
www.oceantwobarbados.com.
Good location on Dover Beach, 88 spacious units on 7 floors with balconies, sleek dark-wood furnishings, giant TVs, and vast walk-in showers; the 1- and 2-bed

apartments have kitchens (everything from gleaming stainless-steel fridges to blenders and washer/dryers) – the higher the floor the better in both standard and views. Nice snake-shaped pool with swim-up bar, rooftop patio, but the breakfast/dinner menu in the restaurant is fairly mediocre; a supermarket is behind the hotel and The Gap is a 10-min walk away. Rates are room-only.

$$$ Silverpoint Hotel
Silver Sands, Christ Church, T420 4416, www.silverpointhotel.com.
Quiet and out of the way on the seafront at Silver Rock Beach between the airport and Oistins, this hotel in elegant buildings with colonial accents has 58 studios and 1- and 2-bed suites with kitchenettes, either with pull-out sofas or lofts for children. Large area of decking for daybeds and sun loungers, small pool, and access to the beach, but the sea is better here for kitesurfing than swimming and is a major area for the sport. Good but expensive restaurant and no alternatives within walking distance, so it's a good idea to have a car.

$$$ South Beach
Rockley Main Rd (Highway 7), Rockley, Christ Church, T435 9441, www.southbeachbarbados.com.
Smart white block with glass balconies next to the Quayside Centre Shopping Plaza and just across the road from Rockley (Accra) Beach and the boardwalk. 49 rooms and suites, newly refurbished in contemporary greys and yellows, sofa-beds, well-equipped kitchens with a welcome pack of basic groceries, the **Swagg Cocktail Lounge & Bistro**, large pool, and friendly and helpful staff. Rates are B&B.

$$$ Southern Palms
St Lawrence Gap, Christ Church, T428 7171, www.southernpalms.net.
A short walk to The Gap and a great location on Dover Beach, this comfortable and unpretentious pink and white hotel has 92 rooms in 6 buildings with balconies/patios and Caribbean-style decor. The spacious suites have kitchenettes and pull-out sofas for children. Very popular with British guests, minimum 5-night stay in high winter season, rates are room-only or B&B. There's a pool and lively beachside restaurant/bar: **The Garden Terrace** (open to all, 1100-2200).

$$$ Yellow Bird Hotel
St Lawrence Gap, Christ Church, T622 8444, www.yellowbirdbarbados.com.
Across the street from the narrow beach at St Lawrence Bay, a 2-min walk to better Worthing Beach and right at the start of The Gap at the western end, 20 2-bed/2-bathroom apartments with balconies, plus 2 studios with rooftop patios that can be combined to make a 3-bed unit, all with pull-out sofas so great value for families/groups, pool and **Cove Bay Café**. Rates are room-only or B&B.

$$ Chateau Blanc Apartments On Sea
1st Av, Worthing, Christ Church, T435 7518, www.chateaublancbarbados.com.
In an excellent location right on Worthing Beach and a 5-min walk to The Gap, the 16 apartments here range from seafront with 1-2 bedrooms with balconies/patios to seaview studios and 4 budget annex rooms with kitchenettes. Simple furnishings and no extras (like a pool or breakfast), but good value, well equipped and with friendly management.

$$-$ Mike's Holiday Apartments/Guesthouse
Landsdown, Silver Sands, Christ Church, T624 4725, www.barbadosmike.com.
Simple accommodation but good value and everything you need for self-catering with good kitchens and bathrooms and patios with dining table and chairs, 2 studios and a 1-bedroom small apartment, no a/c but ceiling fans, steps from the windsurfing/kitesurfing beach, mountain bikes and surfboards available. Friendly family, helpful and informative.

Beach House Cleverdale
4th Av, Worthing, Christ Church, T428 3172,
www.barbados-rentals.com.
Looks like a chattel house from the outside, 15 m from Sandy Beach across a vacant lot and a 5-min walk to St Lawrence Gap, this German-run versatile and affordable guesthouse has 3 double rooms, 2 with bathrooms and 1 with a washbasin, large living/dining room with TV, use of kitchen, veranda and barbecue, also 2 1-bed self-catering studios with separate entrances; you can rent rooms or the whole house, a/c US$5 extra per room per night.

Restaurants

Most restaurants open early in the evening and sitting down to eat a big meal at 1900 or even earlier is quite normal in Barbados. In the peak winter months, make reservations at the smart restaurants a long way in advance; especially for a waterfront or sunset-facing table. Many restaurants automatically add a 10% service charge to the bill, but credit card slips are often left open – beware of tipping twice.

Bridgetown *maps pages 32 and 50.*

$$$ Brown Sugar
Aquatic Gap, off Bay St, on the way to Needham's Point. T426 7684,
www.brownsugarbarbados.net.
All-you-can-eat buffet lunch Sun to Fri 1200-1430, dinner Sat-Sun 1830-2130.
Bajan specialities, with items such as pumpkin fritters, breadfruit, pepperpot, macaroni pie, fish cakes, cou-cou steamed flying fish and some good bread pudding: filling and hearty. The buffets are a great way to try lots of local food, although there's also an à la carte menu for the not so hungry, in an attractive setting with lots of greenery and a waterfall.

$$$ Lobster Alive
Bay St, Brownes Beach, T435 0305,
www.lobsteralive.net. Daily 1200-1600,
Mon-Sat 1800-2100.
Famous for its lobster which you choose from the tank and have cooked fresh to order (it's very expensive and flown in from the Grenadines). But there's also other seafood such as crab backs, conch and chowder. An open relaxed venue on Brownes Beach with sun loungers and umbrellas during the day and great live jazz in the evenings and Sun lunch. Reservations necessary as it gets very busy if a cruise ship is in, with a terribly long wait for food. Could be closed when it's not lobster season and hours are reduced in summer.

$$$-$$ Waterfront Café
Cavans Lane, on the south side of the Careenage, T427 0093, www.waterfrontcafe.com.bb. Mon-Sat 0900-1800, dinner Thu-Sat 1800-2200.
Good but pricey choice of food with both international dishes and local seafood as mains, and more affordable salads, sandwiches and burgers for light meals, and tea and cakes in the afternoon. Great spot to take a break on a walk around Bridgetown with plenty to look at, including art on the walls inside, boats outside in the sunshine or the live band in the evening.

$ Balcony
1st floor, Cave Shepherd Department Store, Broad St, T431 2088. Mon-Fri 1100-1500.
Go early because this is popular with locals and the queue gets long for the buffet lunches. Choose a small or large plate, pile it with salads, macaroni pie and all the trimmings, then pay for your portion of meat or fish and wash it down with a Banks beer. Great place to eat local food at local prices and a good spot for people-watching on Broad St below.

$ Cuz's Fish Stand
Aquatic Gap, off Bay St, on the way to Needham's Point. Daily 0800-1500.
The fish cutter sandwich is a Bajan obsession, and this decades-old clapboard hut on Carlisle Bay is a great place to try one; fried marlin or flying fish in a bread roll with some

salad, cheese and egg optional extras or alternatives, hot sauce and other dressings wash it down with a beer for around US$7. Popular and there's usually a queue at lunchtime. No frills, cash only.

$ Mustors Harbour
McGregor St, T426 5175, see Facebook. Mon-Fri 0830-1545.
This family business has been in operation since 1941 and has a snackette downstairs with Bajan fishcakes, flying fish cutters and other hot snacks, as well as substantial breakfasts, while a more formal restaurant is upstairs for tasty, filling Bajan food like fried or stew chicken with rice and peas, pork chops with macaroni pie or cou-cou and salad.

West coast *map page 50.*

$$$ Cin Cin By The Sea
Prospect, St James, T424 4557, www.cincinbarbados.com. Mon-Fri 1130-1500, daily 1800-2300.
Close to Batts Rock and Paradise Beach, and one of Barbados' most fashionable restaurants where you can dine either in a/c with a view of the sea through giant glass windows or on an open-air terrace over the ocean. Inventive dishes with lots of interesting combinations on the plate such as gnocchi and jerk pork in a sweet pea sauce or king fish with asparagus and roasted peppers. Reservations are essential if you want a good table.

$$$ The Cliff & The Cliff Beach Club
Highway 1, Derricks, St James, T432 1922, www.thecliffbarbados.com. Dinner only, Mon-Sat from 1800, bar opens until 2400, plus Sun in winter season, reservations essential.
One of Barbados' best restaurants and worth the exorbitant prices to sit at a waterfront table on the torch-lit decks to see the rays and tarpon swim up to the lights for feeding and a glimpse of the theatrical decor. The food is equally memorable, both for its beautiful presentation and flavours, especially the creative desserts. Prices are

set US$133 for 2 courses and US$155 for 3, but an excellent venue to celebrate a special occasion in style. The more casual (though still pricey) **Cliff Beach Club** (T432 0797, www.thecliffbeachclub.com, Mon-Sat 1130-2300, Sun 1130-1430) has 4 sea-facing decks under white sails, a good menu from tuna salads to oysters, a trendy bar hung with glitter balls, and live music some evenings and at lunchtime on Sun.

$$$ Daphne's
Highway 1, Payne's Bay, St James, T432 2731, www.eleganthotels.com/daphnes. Daily 1830-2200, bar from 1700.
Set directly behind Paynes Bay Beach between Elegant Hotels' **The House** and **Tamarind**, chic and contemporary and a long-established West Coast favourite with Italian, vegetarian and gluten-free menus, signature dishes include lobster and sea bass, ask for a table by the waterfront when you book, and arrive early for a drink in the cocktail bar at happy hour (1700-1900).

$$$ Lone Star
See Where to stay, page 82. Daily, breakfast 0830-1030, lunch 1130-1500, dinner 1830-2300.
This super-chic upmarket restaurant is a favourite on the Platinum Coast and has a large deck spreading on to the sand with overhead fans, giant mirrors, artwork, stylish blue and white decor and a sophisticated cocktail lounge. The menu is generally European with steaks, lamb and duck plus local seafood and the lunchtime menu offers lighter meals such as catch of the day or wood-fired pizza.

$$$ The Mews
2nd St, Holetown, T432 1122, www.themewsbarbados.com. Mon-Thu 1730-2300, Fri-Sat 1730-1200.
Quite expensive but superb food with a mix of local and French dishes, served in a very pretty house with contemporary art on the walls, tables upstairs on the balcony or interior patio, and a lively bar with a tapas menu downstairs and live music on Fri nights.

$$ The Tides
Balmore House, Holetown, St James,
T432 8356, www.tidesbarbados.com.
Sun-Fri 1200-1430, daily 1800-2300.
This waterfront restaurant offers a fine-dining menu of seafood with Asian touches, meat and vegetarian dishes, decadent desserts, all served on a magical terrace with a boardwalk between the tables and the sea and trees growing through the roof of the building. Arrive early for drinks at the bar which doubles up as an art gallery.

$$$-$$ The Fish Pot
At Little Good Harbour, see Where to stay, page 81. Daily by reservation only, breakfast 0800-1000, lunch 1200-1500, dinner 1800-2200.
Located in 18th-century Fort Rupert directly on the water's edge with coral stone walls, an open-air terrace and imaginative menu. Standout items include lobster ravioli, pan-fried mahi mahi and oven-roasted sea bass. After breakfast/lunch you can swim, and at dinner book a table overlooking the ocean for an amazing sunset view.

$$ Mullins Beach Bar
Highway 1B, Mullins, just south of Speightstown, St Peter, T422 2044, see Facebook. Open for food Mon-Sat 1000-1900, Sun 1000-1600; bar stays open later.
Upmarket beach bar with a bright and buzzy atmosphere and an all-day menu for beach goers with service to your sun bed. Serves local dishes such as curry, roti and flying fish, plus salads, seafood and burgers, a great spot to watch the sunset; regular barbecues, music evenings and sporting events shown on big-screen TV.

$$-$ Patisserie & Bistro Flindt
1st St, Holetown, St James, T432 2626, www.flindtbarbados.com. Mon-Fri 0800-1700, Sat 0730-1400, Sun 0730-1200.
The cakes, desserts and sweets in the patisserie are divine but pricey and the handmade chocolates are out of this world. Sandwiches, salads and pasta are on offer at lunchtime and they do a full English breakfast. Picnics can be made to order, ideal for an event such as the **Holders Season** (see page 13).

$ Fisherman's Pub
Queen's St, Speightstown, St Peter, T422 2703, see Facebook. Mon-Sat 1100-1800.
A Speightstown institution which first opened to provide snacks and meals to local fishermen and is now a deservedly popular lunch stop for tourists on island tours with tables on a seafront terrace. Good Bajan food includes cou-cou, fish head soup with dumplings, fried flying fish and sweet potato pie, all at very reasonable prices and served buffet-style at busier lunchtimes.

East coast *map page 50.*

$$$ Atlantis Hotel
See Where to stay, page 84. Daily 0800-1000, 1200-1530, Mon-Sat 1700-2000.
Famous for its Bajan buffet lunches on Wed and Sun which might feature conch (lambi) fritters, jerk pork, curried yam or goat, rotis, pepperpot stew or flying fish cutters, while at other times and at dinner is a sophisticated menu of seafood, duck, beef and good vegetarian options such as quinoa and couscous salads. Great east coast views from the breezy terrace.

$$ Naniki
Surinam, St Joseph, T433 1300, www.nanikiretreats.sba.bb. Daily 1230-1530.
Perched high in the hills overlooking the Atlantic coast, Naniki is difficult to get to but well worth the effort; turn off Highway 3 just south of St Joseph's church at the sign to Lush Life Nature Resort. A Bajan lunch of grilled seafood, poultry or pork served with local favourites like yam, breadfruit and sweet potato, is served with a great view over fields and palm trees from the deck; jazz brunch buffet lunch on Sun, a special place run by Tom Hinds who also rents out cottages on the property. *Naniki* is an Arawak word meaning 'spirited' or 'full of life'.

$$ Round House Inn
See Where to stay, page 84. Nov-Apr, daily 0830-2000, May-Oct lunch only 1130-1600.
Lovely location overlooking the Atlantic and pounding surf with fresh ocean breezes from the terrace, very popular for lunch on island tours. A long menu of Caribbean and international features everything from fish cakes and club sandwiches to cheeseburgers and catch of the day. There's a good choice of wines and cocktails plus live music at the weekend.

South coast *map page 50.*

$$$ Café Luna
At Little Arches Boutique Hotel, see Where to stay, page 85, T428 6172, www.cafeluna barbados.com. Daily1800-2200, by reservation only.
Fine dining on the rooftop terracotta terrace of this charming hotel with a superb changing menu of Caribbean, Asian and Mediterranean dishes created by acclaimed Canadian chef Mark de Gruchy (or Moo as he is better known). Very romantic and atmospheric, impeccable service, ocean views over Enterprise (Miami) Beach, sushi specials on Thu and Fri nights, go early for sundowner cocktails.

$$$ Champers
Skeetes Hill, Christ Church, T434 3463, www.champersbarbados.com. Sun-Fri 1130-1500, daily 1800-2130.
Overlooking Rockley (Accra) Beach, this, one of the best restaurants on the south coast, offers waterfront dining on the terrace or upstairs on a balcony. They serve very good food with some interesting combinations of flavours; the seafood is especially varied (from lobster to lion fish), portions are generous and the service excellent. Reservations are essential for a good table.

$$$ Coral Reef Club
See Where to stay, above. Daily 1300-1430, 1930-2130, by reservation only.
Elegant dining in this top-notch, 5-star hotel where the restaurant, on an oceanfront covered terrace, offers a daily changing à la carte menu, mostly French cuisine infused with local Caribbean ingredients. There's live music most nights, a Bajan/international buffet on Mon night, a barbecue on Thu night followed by a floor show featuring limbo dancing, folk dancing and fire-eating.

$$$-$$ Tapas
Hastings Main Rd, Hastings, Christ Church, T228 0704, www.tapasbarbados.com. Mon-Fri 1130-2230, Sat-Sun 1130-2400.
Right alongside the South Coast Boardwalk, this buzzy restaurant and bar has a breezy deck and a menu of substantial and varied Caribbean/Asian/Mediterranean tapas such as spicy Thai fish cakes, smoked marlin, meatballs or shark fritters, more expensive full meals, all beautifully presented and with good service and the bar stays open late at the weekends. Reservations are recommended for a table by the boardwalk.

$$ Café Sol
St Lawrence Gap, Christ Church, T420 7655, www.cafesolbarbados.com. Mon 1730-2230, Tue-Sun 1130-2230.
This Mexican restaurant at the western end of The Gap is famous for its 15 flavours of margaritas (by the glass or jug), and has a menu of all the usual TexMex dishes such as nachos, fajitas, tacos and chimichangas, and there's often a party mood.

$$ Naru Restaurant & Lounge
Hastings Main Rd, Hastings, Christ Church, T228 6278, www.narubarbados.com. Tue-Sat 1800-2130.
Popular and casual spot also on the South Coast Boardwalk with sea views, open kitchen, modern decor, engaging staff and a menu that blends Caribbean cuisine with sushi and traditional Japanese dishes – there's something for everybody, from pork chops and sweet potato mash to bento boxes and maki rolls. Well-priced and also does takeaway.

Just Grillin'
Quayside Centre, Rockley, Christ Church,
T435 6469, www.justgrillinbarbados.com.
Mon-Sat 1130-2200, Sun 1730-2200.
Open-sided eatery where you place your
order at a window, wait to be called, then eat
at shared wooden tables. Options include
huge portions of steak, ribs, chicken and
fish served with vegetables, salad, rice or
potatoes; also sandwiches and serves alcohol.

$ Surfers Café
Oistin's Main Rd, Oistins, Christ Church,
T420 9283, www.surferscafebarbados.com.
Wed 0730-2400, Thu-Fri 0730-1500,
Sat-Sun 0730-2300.
On the western side of Oistins opposite
the Massy supermarket and with a balcony
overlooking the bay, a laid-back café/bar,
good service and food, cooked breakfasts,
salads, grilled catch of the day from Oistins
fish market, coffees and drinks and liveliest
from 1930 on Wed and Sun when bands play.

Bars and clubs

Barbados is lively after dark, and nightlife
ranges from no-frills rum shops and sports
bars, to flashy cocktail bars, nightclubs
and dinner shows. On the south coast at
St Lawrence Gap is a concentration of bars
and clubs in close proximity to each other,
while on the west coast is a clutch of rather
more salubrious bars on 1st St and 2nd St in
the heart of Holetown, but every hotel has
a bar and rum shops are found even in the
tiniest settlement. The biggest street party
on the island is the Oistins Fish Fry; see box,
page 76.

Bert's Bar
Rockley Main Rd, Christ Church, T435 7924,
www.bertsbarbados.com. Daily 1100-0100.
Across the road from Rockley (Accra)
Beach, this casual spot is a combination of
a sports bar and family restaurant and has
been in operation since the 1970s. Outside
decks and swimming pools, a menu
of inexpensive burgers, pizzas and fish

platters, and is well known for its delicious
(and potent) banana daiquiris.

Bubba's Sports Bar & Restaurant
Rockley Main Rd, Christ Church, T435 8731,
www.bubbassportsbar.net. Mon-Thu 1130-
2300, Fri-Sat 1100-0100, Sun 0800-2300.
A cavernous bar famous for its 3 10-ft screens
plus 17 other TVs for watching sports –
British soccer, NBA basketball, NFL Football,
Formula One – while you eat and drink. Also
offers a Sun buffet breakfast.

Cove
St Lawrence Gap, Christ Church, T420 7612,
www.coveclubbarbados.com. Mon-Sat
2100-0400, Sun 2100-2400.
Classic large nightclub on The Gap attracting
a youthful crowd, locals and holidaymakers,
indoor and outdoor dance floors, plenty of
drinks specials and a wide range of music,
from reggae and calypso to mainstream pop.

Drift Ocean Terrace Lounge
Highway 1, opposite the Chattel Village,
Holetown, St James, T432 2808, www.
driftinbarbados.com. Daily 1700-0200.
Lovely location on the waterfront with tables
on a deck overlooking the sea or inside in a/c
lounge with local and international artwork
on the walls. Excellent cocktails, good winelist
and 'night bites' including sushi, Bajan fish
cakes and mini-burgers served individually
or on platters to share. Popular any night but
lively after work on Fri with DJ music.

Harbour Lights
Bay St, St Michael, T436 7225, www.harbour
lightsbarbados.com. Nightclub Wed 2100-
0200, Fri 2130-0300, dinner and show Mon
and Wed 1900-2230.
An open-air venue on the beach at Carlisle
Bay that is popular with locals, tourists and
expats and is always pumping with music,
lively and crowded. The Mon and Wed beach
party includes barbecue dinner, drinks and
show featuring fire eaters, stilt walkers,
acrobats, limbo dancers and a finale of steel
pan and dancers. It is suitable for families

early on (before the nightclub) and includes hotel transfers there and back.

John Moore Bar
Highway 1B, Weston, St James, T422 2258. Daily 1000-2300.
Of the many hundreds of rum shops on Barbados this one has a fantastic location and is popular with both locals and visitors. The main bar fronts the west coast road, but makeshift tables in a ramshackle building out the back are right over a little stretch of un-touristy beach. Friendly, plenty of Mount Gay rum, and a bus stop outside.

The Lime Bar
Limegrove Lifestyle Centre, Holetown, St James, T271 8261, www.limebarbarbados. com. Sun-Tue 1000-0200, Wed-Thu 1000-1500, Fri and Sat 1000-0400.
Situated in an al fresco courtyard at the extravagant Limegrove Lifestyle Centre, a popular (some might say pretentious) west coast spot offering a vast choice of expensive cocktails, wines, cognacs, gins and whiskies, plus regular live music and DJs. **Zoola Café** is part of The Lime Bar and serves coffees, breakfasts, pastries and cakes from 0900.

MOJO Bar & The Chopping Board Kitchen
Worthing Main Rd, Worthing, Christ Church, T435 9008, see Facebook. Daily 1000-0300.
One of the most established bars on the south coast with pictures of musicians decorating the walls and a back room is devoted to Bob Marley. Excellent cocktails and good food at the adjoining Chopping Board Kitchen, including gourmet burgers, steaks, fish, pasta and other dishes at reasonable prices (kitchen closes at 2300 but late-night snacks are available).

The Old Jamm Inn
St Lawrence Gap, Christ Church, T428 3919, see Facebook. Daily 1800-0300/0400.
A popular spot on The Gap offering "booze, beats and burgers", this lounge bar with outdoor deck delivers good food to go with the music and drinks. Live and DJ music,

sometimes jazz, sometimes reggae, and plenty of people dancing.

Red Door Lounge
At the end of 2nd St, Holetown, St James, T620 3761, www.reddoorbarbados.com, see Facebook for what's on. Mon-Thu 1900-2400, Fri-Sat 1900-0400.
Good and varied cocktails and tapas, live entertainment and music, including piano, DJs play the classics, latest hits and mixes; a good time is had by all. The club attracts locals, tourists and celebrities, it's busy but friendly and service is good, while the decor is modern and funky.

Scarlet
Paynes Bay, St James, T432 3663, www. scarletbarbados.com. Tue-Sat 1700-2400.
A chic cocktail bar/restaurant in a chattel house on the road behind Paynes Bay with scarlet and black decor and pop art of Marilyn Monroe and Jackie Kennedy. Long list of interesting cocktails (mojitos are a speciality), Asian/Bajan light bites as well as full meals.

Sugar Ultra Lounge
St Lawrence Gap, Christ Church, T420 7662, www.sugarbarbados.com. Thu and Sat 1000-0400.
Miami-style club with light show wall, VIP areas and white leather sofas. DJs play a good mix of dancehall, pop, soca and hip hop. Professionally managed with an upmarket feel but drinks are expensive and the large venue is difficult to fill sometimes.

Entertainment

Cinemas
Globe Drive-In, *Adams Castle, not far from Sheraton Mall, off Tom Adams Highway, Christ Church, T437 0480, www.globedrivein.com. Daily 1830 and 2100.* Drive-in with 2 movies nightly and a canteen and bar.
Limegrove Cinemas, *Limegrove Lifestyle Centre, Holetown, St James, T271-0071, www. limegrovecinemas.com. Daily 1000-2200.* A luxury cinema with large leather seats and table service for drinks and snacks.

Olympus Theatres, *Sheraton Mall, Sargeants Village, Christ Church, T228 5255, www. olympus.bb. Daily 1530-2130.* A 6-screen multiplex with snack bar.

Shopping

Barbados has some of the best shopping in the Caribbean and, although prices are high, the range of goods available is excellent, Duty-free shopping for jewellery, cosmetics, perfumes, electronics and designer goods and the like is well advertised with discounts of 30-50% – you need to present your passport, airline ticket or (if on a cruise) travel documents at the point of sale. A duty-free shopping centre for cruise ship passengers is at the Bridgetown Cruise Terminal and there are duty-free outlets at Grantley Adams International Airport. **Cave Shephard** (www. mycaveshepherd.com) is a duty-free chain of shops with its main department store on Broad St in Bridgetown and other outlets in shopping centres and some of the large resorts. **Broad St** and **Swan St** are the main shopping areas in the centre of Bridgetown, and there are a number of modern malls around the island.

Art galleries

Barbados Arts Council, *Pelican Craft Centre, Harbour Rd, Bridgetown, T426 4385, www.the barbados artscouncil.com. Daily 1000-1700.* A non-profit organization set up to foster Barbadian art and artists. Works exhibited at these galleries are drawn from its 300 members, both established artists with an international reputation and those just starting out.

Gallery of Caribbean Art, *Northern Business Centre, Queen's St, Speightstown, St Peter, T419 0858, www.artgallerycaribbean. com. Mon-Fri 1000-1600, Sat 1000-1400.* A range of contemporary art, sculpture and photography from all around the Caribbean.

On The Wall Art Gallery, *at Champers, see Restaurants, above, www.onthewallartgallery. com. Open restaurant hours, daily 1200-1600, 1900-2300.* A fine art and craft gallery dedicated to showcasing local artists of varying styles and mediums. There's another outlet at **Earthworks Pottery** (below).

Queen's Park Gallery, *Pelican Craft Centre, Princess Alice Highway, Bridgetown, T427 2345. Mon-Fri 0900-1600, Sat 0900-1400.* This gallery was originally located at The Queen's House in Queen's Park, but is now at the Pelican Craft Centre. Run by the National Cultural Foundation, it exhibits and sells paintings, sculptures, prints and other work from emerging and established Barbadian artists.

Crafts

Best of Barbados, *Chattel Village in Holetown, Southern Palms Hotel in St Lawrence Gap, Quayside Centre Shopping Plaza in Rockley, the airport departure lounge and the Bridgetown Cruise Terminal, www.best-of-barbados.com.* The ultimate gift shop with every Barbados souvenir imaginable. The designs mostly stem from the work of Jill Walker, who has been living and painting in Barbados since 1956, and they have a network of cottage workers making things exclusively for the shop. Her prints of local scenes are on sale, as well as mugs, candles and T-shirts.

Earthworks Pottery, *Edgehill Heights No 2, St Thomas, T425 0223, www.earthworks-pottery.com. Mon-Fri 0900-1700, Sat 0900-1300.* A large showroom of desirable hand-decorated bowls, pots, jugs and tableware (the coffee pots in the shape of Bajan chattel houses are fun), everything is handmade and you can see the potters at work. Next door is a 2nd branch of **On The Wall Art Gallery** (see above), a **Batik Studio**, the **Ins and Outs Gift Emporium** which sells locally produced condiments, linens, soaps and crafts, and there's a café.

Pelican Craft Centre, *Princess Alice Highway, between Bridgetown Cruise Terminal and Princess Alice Bus Terminal, Bridgetown, T622 1683. Mon-Fri 0900-1800, Sat 0900-1400.* Good displays of craft items, all made in Barbados, at over 25 shops in replica chattel houses selling local art, pottery, woodwork, glass products and clothes. You can watch the artisans in the workshops and there's a café.

Food

There are many supermarkets, convenience stores and farmers' markets. Nearly all food is imported, so is generally expensive. There are several village fish markets around the island, where you can get fish cleaned and filleted by the vendors.

Cheapside Public Market, *Cheapside Rd, Bridgetown, T426 4463. Mon-Sat 0700-1700.* Bridgetown's main market is good for fruit and vegetables and is a colorful place to visit (see page 31).

The Green Monkey Chocolatier, *Worthing Main Rd (Highway 7), Worthing, Christ Church, T435 5567. Tue-Fri 1000-1800, Sat 1000-1600; and Limegrove Lifestyle Centre, Holetown, St James, T427 5567, Mon-Fri 1000-1900, Sat 1100-1800; www.thegreenmonkeychocolatier.com.* Expensive but deliciously decadent hand-crafted artisanal chocolates, salted caramels, rum truffles, French macarons filled with ganache, chocolate-dipped marshmallows and jams and marmalades. The Limegrove branch has a small café serving coffee, gourmet teas, hot chocolate and champagne.

Hastings Farmer's Market, *ArtSplash Centre, Highway 7, Hastings, Christ Church, T228 0776, www.hastingsfarmersmarket.com. Wed, Sat and Sun 0800-1400.* Organic fruit, vegetables and eggs, freshly baked breads and pastries, prepared Bajan meals, plus arts and crafts and handmade soaps and lotions. The **ArtSplash Centre** (www.artsplashbarbados.com) has a children's play park with 2 zip-lines and a café, and there's free entry on market days.

Holders Farmers Market, *Holders House, Holders Hill, St James, T844 1729, www.holdersfarmersmarket.com. Sun 0900-1400.* Set in the grounds of the beautiful historic Holders House (see page 47) and overlooking one of the Sandy Lane golf courses, stalls sell arts and crafts, organic farm produce, and food products such as gourmet cheeses, jams, jellies and chutneys.

Jordan's Supermarket, *www.jordanssupermarket.com.* The other good supermarket chain with 4 branches: Speightstown, Fitts Village, and Baxters Rd and Fairchild St in Bridgetown. Mon-Thu 0800-2100, Fri-Sat 0800-2200.

Massy Stores Supermarket, *www.massystores.com/bb.* The biggest of the chain supermarkets (they are Caribbean-wide), always well stocked and have bakeries, deli counters and pharmacies. The larger branches are in Holetown, Oistins, Warrens, Worthing, Six Cross Roads, Sheraton Mall and Sky Mall. Mon-Thu 0800-2000, Fri-Sat 0800-2100, Sun 0900-1400.

Shopping malls

Limegrove Lifestyle Centre, *Highway 1, Holetown, St James, T620 5463, www.limegrove.com. Mon-Sat 1000-1900, Sun 1100-1800.* An attractive and upscale complex with shops selling luxury brands, as well as cafés, bars, a cinema, art gallery and spa.

Sheraton Mall, *Sargeants Village, Christ Church, T437 0970, www.sheratonmall.com. Mon-Sat 0900-2100.* Immediately off the ABC Highway, the largest mall on the island with over 120 shops, banks, a food court and a multiplex cinema. Roughly a 10-min drive north of St Lawrence Gap, the mall offers a free shuttle service from hotels on the south coast (phone to organize pick-up) and it's on several bus routes.

Sky Mall, *Haggatt Hall, St Michael, T431 6850, www.skymall.bb. Mon-Sat 0900-2100, Sun 1000-2000.* At the JTC Ramsay roundabout on the ABC Highway, also known as the Bussa roundabout after the large statue there. An assortment of general shops, a food court and a large branch of **Massy Stores Supermarket**.

What to do

Cricket

Kensington Oval, *President Kennedy Dr, Bridgetown, T537 1600, www.kensingtonoval.org.* Cricket in the Caribbean is a game played to a backdrop of rapturous music and joyous partying, and in front of the world's most knowledgeable spectators, who will stop you in the street to provide a breakdown of tactics and techniques (or their absence) in West Indian batting. In Barbados the historic Oval was established in 1882 when **Pickwick Cricket Club** leased 1.6 ha (4 acres) of pasture from Kensington Plantation and developed a cricket ground with a clubhouse. It first hosted a Test Match in 1930 when the West Indies and England played to a draw, and had a major upgrade for the ICC Cricket World Cup in 2007 to add extra seats and improve facilities for the players, media and sponsors. The current capacity is 11,000 spectators and there's also a large grassy hill for fans to have picnics on. For information on fixtures, check the websites of the **Barbados Cricket Association** (www.bcacricket.org) or the **West Indies Cricket Board** (www.windiescricket.com).

Cycling

Bike Caribbean, *Mirabelle Apartments, St Lawrence Gap, Christ Church, T622 2056, www.bikecaribbeantours.com*. Run by Randy Licorish who can organize mountain bike tours just about anywhere on the island from 2-6 hrs and from beginner to advanced level; US$65-120 per person. Examples are along the cliffs and bays on the extreme north coast; a combination of hiking and biking along the old railway track on the east coast; or a gentler ride alongside the south coast beaches. Also rents out mountain bikes, road bikes and kids' bikes from the shop in St Lawrence Gap from US$20 a day with helmets; weekly rates available and can deliver.

Diving

For the best dive locations, see Planning, page 17. Scuba diving to reefs or wrecks around the coast can be arranged with a number of companies on the south and west coasts. Most will organize transfers from hotels. Expect to pay in the region of

US$75 for a 1-tank dive, US$125 for a 2-tank dive, US$85 for a night dive, US$100 for a PADI Discover Scuba course, and US$430-460 for a PADI Open Water course. In the event of a diving emergency, the Barbados hyperbaric chamber is at the Barbados Defence Force Headquarters, St Ann's Fort, Bridgetown, T436 5483.

Barbados Blue, *Hilton Barbados Resort, Needham's Point, Bridgetown, T434 5734, www.divebarbadosblue.com*.

The Dive Shop Ltd, *Ameys Alley, off Bay St, Bridgetown, T426 9947, www.thediveshopbarbados.com*.

Eco Dive Barbados, *Cavens Lane, Bridgetown, T243 5816, www.ecodivebarbados.com*.

Hightide Watersports, *Coral Reef Club, Porters, Highway 1, Holetown, St James, T432 0931, www.divehightide.com*.

Reefers and Wreckers, *Queen's St, Speightstown, St Peter, T422 5450, www.scubadiving.bb*.

Roger's Scuba Shack, *Bay St, Bridgetown, T436 3483, www.rogersscubashack.com*.

West Side Scuba Centre, *Mowbray, Hastings Main Rd, Christ Church, T262 1029, www.westsidescuba.com*.

Fishing

The waters off the coast of Barbados offer ideal for fishing barracuda, blue marlin, yellow fin tuna, white marlin, sailfish, wahoo and dolphin fish (mahi mahi). Fishing is particularly good Jan-Apr when all these game fish are in season. Charter boats for game fishing are lined up along the Careenage, Bridgetown, so you can inspect the goods before deciding who to call. Trips include all tackle and bait, drinks and snacks, lunch on the full-day trips, and some organize a stop on a beach or a swim with the turtles. For 4 people, expect to pay in the region of US$350 for 4 hrs, US$450 for 6 hrs and US$650 for 8 hrs.

Barbados Game Fishing Association (BGFA), *www.barbadosgamefishing.com*. Runs all the game fishing events in Barbados including the **Barbados International Game Fishing Tournament** in Mar/Apr at Port St Charles.

Golf

An 18-hole round can cost from US$120 to US$200 and more, but most clubs offer 3- to 7-day deals for people on holiday and there are low-season and group discounts.

Apes Hill Club, *Apes Hill, St James, T432 4500, www.apeshillclub.com*. A beautiful and challenging par-72 championship course high up in the hills with a tremendous view of the west coast and an upmarket country club with restaurant, pro shop, gym and 2 swimming pools.

Barbados Golf Club, *Durants, Christ Church T428 8463, www.barbadosgolfclub.com*. A public par-72 18-hole course with 5 lakes; a 5-min drive from Oistins on Highway 7, so handy for most of the south coast.

Rockley Golf & Country Club, *Rockley, Christ Church, T435 7873, www.rockleygolfclub.com*. An informal and inexpensive 9-hole course, every Sat is a competition which is open to members and visitors, clubhouse with bar and restaurant, pro shop with club hire.

Royal Westmoreland, *Westmoreland, St James, T419 7242, www.royalwestmoreland. com*. An 18-hole, par-72 course spread over 194 ha (480 acres) on a hilly site with views over the west coast. To play here you must be staying in one of the villas or at a hotel with an access agreement or be the guest of a member. For non-residents/guests limited tee times are available 1000-1100. Clubhouse, pro shop and driving range.

Sandy Lane, *St James, T444 2514, www. sandylane.com*. 3 golf courses; the 9-hole **Old Nine**, and the Tom Fazio designed 18-hole **Country Club** and **Green Monkey**, the latter is carved from an old stone quarry and is exclusive to Sandy Lane guests only. Golf carts are fitted with GPS, there are caddies, driving range and a fine clubhouse and restaurant where Tiger Woods got married in 2004.

Hiking

Barbados may not be very high, but there are numerous opportunities to hike unguided through sugar cane fields, gullies, rural communities and isolated coasts. A recommended hike is along part of the old railway line on the east coast (see box, page 66).

Barbados National Trust, *T426 2421, www. barbadosnationaltrust.org*. Organizes 3-hr Sun hikes at 0600 and 1530, and moonlight hikes at 1730 or 1800 (depending on the month). Groups are separated into 3 speeds or capabilities: 'stop and stare', 8-10 km, 'here and there', 13-15 km, and 'grin and bear', 19-21 km. All these hikes are free but donations to the Barbados National Trust are welcome. They start from various locations around the island, and you can pick up a schedule from the office in Wildey (see page 80) or they are posted on the website of the **Barbados Hiking Association**; www. barbadoshikingassociation.com.

Hike Barbados, *T230 4818, www. hikebarbados.com and Facebook*. Highly regarded and entertaining Stephen Mendes offers enjoyable guided scenic walks of 3-16 km for US$200-250, regardless of the numbers of hikers. He customizes the hikes to skill level and knows Barbados intimately.

Ocean Echo Stables, *New Castle, St John, T433 6772, www.barbadoshorseriding.com*. As well as horse riding (below) the stables can organize guided hiking along the east coast: a moderate 2-3 hrs following the old railway line from Martin's Bay up to Bath Beach or Conset Bay, US$45-55, or a more challenging 2½ hrs from the top of Hackleton's Cliff down to Martin's Bay, US$50. Picnics can be provided and transfers from hotels organized.

Horse riding

Ocean Echo Stables, *New Castle, St John, T433 6772, www.barbadoshorseriding.com*. Offers a number of rides along the east coast from US$70 for 1 hr down to Bath Beach suitable for beginners, to US$125 for 3 hrs that includes Bath Beach, Codrington College and farm trails down to Conset Bay for those experienced in the saddle. There's also a 1½-hr full moon ride; US$100. Picnics can be provided and transfers from hotels organized.

Polo

The first polo match in Barbados was played in 1884; British cavalry officers had brought the sport with them and it was a game that suited the Bajan lifestyle as a number of wealthy plantation owners had their own stables. Matches were originally played at the Garrison Savannah but there are now several polo fields on the island. It remains the sport of the affluent elite but, like horse racing (see box, page 39), polo is a wonderful afternoon's entertainment for spectators. The season starts just after Christmas and runs through to May, when teams from all over the world visit Barbados. You can watch the game while sipping a cup of tea or a glass of wine and there is always a lively lime afterwards. There are usually 2 matches held from about 1500 on match days; admission is around US$10, children (under 12) US$5.

Apes Hill Polo Club, *Apes Hill, St James, T262 3282, www.apeshillpolo.com.*

Barbados Polo Club, *Holders Hill, St James, T432 1802, www.barbadospoloclub.com, also see Facebook for fixtures.*

Lion Castle Polo Club, *on the Lion Castle Polo Estate, St Thomas, T622 7656, see Facebook for fixtures.*

Running

Barbados Hash House Harriers, *www.barbadoshash.com.* Every Sat the Hash (sometimes 100-strong) have a 1- to 2-hr fun run/walk starting form a different location each week, followed by a barbecue and drinks or a meal at a beach bar. Events are posted on the website and there is a US$0.50 fee for participating.

Run Barbados Marathon, *www.run barbados.org.* Held over a weekend in early Dec, open to all and attracting a number of international competitors, this consist of a 'Fun Mile', 5 km, 10 km, a half marathon, and a full individual and relay team marathon. The start and finish point is the Bay Street Esplanade overlooking Carlisle Bay. Fees for visitors range from U$20-85.

Sailing

A number of outfits in Bridgetown offer lunchtime and sunset cruises on sleek catamarans, many of which are based at the Careenage while others are at Shallow Draught near the Bridgetown Cruise Terminal. If you pre-book, transport from hotels is included in the rates. Each takes a maximum of 12-14 for a comfortable and friendly tour of the west coast, stopping to snorkel over a couple of wrecks and swimming with turtles. Lunch cruises usually go from 0930 and return at 1430 and cost in the region of US$110-120, children (3-12) US$85-95, under 3s free. They include a Bajan-style buffet lunch and unlimited drinks, including rum punch. Sunset cruises are 1500-1900, US$95-135/US$55-85 depending on the type of meal you get – finger food or a full dinner plus drinks. There's also the option of booking a private charter for families/groups.

Calabaza Sailing Cruises Barbados, *at the Careenage, Bridgetown, T826 4048, www.sailcalabaza.com.*

Cool Runnings Catamaran Cruises, *at the Careenage, Bridgetown, T436 0911, www.silvermoonbarbados.com.*

Elegance Catamaran Cruises, *at the Careenage, Bridgetown, T830 4218, www.elegancebarbados.com.*

El Tigre Catamaran Sailing Cruises, *at the Careenage, Bridgetown, T417 7245, www.eltigrecruises.com.*

Silver Moon Catamaran Cruises, *Shallow Draught, Bridgetown, T435 5285, www.silvermoonbarbados.com.*

Tiami Catamaran Cruises, *Shallow Draught, Bridgetown, T430 0900, www.tiamicatamarancruises.com.*

Black Pearl Jolly Roger Party Cruises, *Carlisle House, Bridgetown, T436 2885, www.barbadosblackpearl-jollyroger1.com.* Rather than a catamaran, this option is on a pirate boat and offers 4-hr daytime and evening cruises along the west coast with food, unlimited drinks, activities like rope-swinging or walking the plank, music and dancing, and on the evening cruise entertainment includes limbo dancing, stilt walkers, and the opportunity to get dressed up in pirate costumes. It's fun for adults and children; prices start from US$87, children (4-12) US$45 including transfers.

Stand-up paddle boarding (SUP)

SUPing has taken off in Barbados in a big way and there are lots of good locations for the sport in the quieter bays of the south and west coasts. Many of the resorts have boards for their guests and it's great for all ages and beginners.

Paddle Barbados, *Barbados Cruising Club, Bay St, Bridgetown, T249 2787, www.paddle barbados.com*. Rents out boards for US$20 per 2 hrs, which includes brief instruction, and also offers SUP lessons and a tour in Carlisle Bay, 1½ hrs US$60; for an extra US$10 you get snorkelling gear to jump off and snorkel over the shipwrecks. Sometimes available are SUP yoga sessions for US$40. Also rents out snorkelling gear, boogie boards and inflatable kayaks from their base at the **Barbados Cruising Club**, and delivers/picks up SUPs and regular surf boards to your hotel if you want to rent for a few days; from US$30 per day.

Submarines

Atlantis Submarines Barbados, *Shallow Draft Harbour, off Spring Garden Highway, 1.3 km north of Bridgetown Cruise Terminal, Bridgetown, T436 8929, www.barbados. atlantissubmarines.com*. Multiple departures daily – check website for times, daytime tour US$111.50, children (13-17) US$54.50 (12 and under, but above 1 m tall) US$35, night tour US$121.50/US$59.60/US$38, discounts in low season and for online booking, hotel transfers US$10 per person. For those who want to see the underwater world without getting wet, a voyage on the 48-seater, a/c, port-holed Atlantis Submarine is an expensive but thrilling alternative and great for kids. The craft submerges around 45 m to the ocean

bed; the submarine's day dives concentrate on the numerous fish, turtles and reef life and takes you to a shipwreck, while the night one also illuminates the corals and predator fish with coloured spotlights. The whole trip lasts 1 hr 45 mins, but begins with a short video and then the boat ride from the dock to the submarine and back, so the underwater time is about 40-45 mins.

Surfing

For the best surf spots, see Planning, page 19. For further information on surfing events in Barbados, check the website or the Facebook page of the **Barbados Surfing Association** (www.barbadossurfingassociation.org). Most of the surf schools on the island are mobile; they take you to where the waves are best. Surfing lessons are usually somewhere along the south coast, and free south coast hotel pick-ups are often included. Most offer 2-hr group lessons, daily in the morning and afternoon, US$60-80, and packages of 3 lessons and a board for a week, US$160-180. All offer board rentals for around US$15 per 2-hrs, US$20-30 per day and US$100-150 per week (price depends on whether they are fun short boards or quality long boards) and some operators will deliver to your accommodation. Check with your airline how much it costs to bring your board with you to Barbados and compare costs. For repairs and to buy or rent gear, the **Dread or Dead Surf Shop** is on Hastings Main Rd (Highway 7) Christ Church, T228 4785, www.dreadordead.com, daily 0900-1600.

Barry's Surf Barbados, *T256 3906, www.boosyssurfschool.com*.
Boosy's Surf School, *T267 3182, www.boosyssurfschool.com*.
Burkie's Surf School, *T230 2456, www.blog.surfbarbados.net*.
Ride the Tide Surf School, *T234 2361, www.ridethetidebarbados.com*.
SurfInBarbados Surf School, *T228 4785, www.surfinbarbados.com*.
Zed's Surfing Adventures, *T262 7873, www.zedssurftravel.com*.

Tour operators

Cruise ship passengers are given a taste of the island by being whisked round in about 6 hrs. These tours include a stop at the viewpoint on Cherry Tree Hill, a drive through the Scotland District, a stop on the beach at Bathsheba on the east coast and at St John's Church, and then perhaps a visit to the Flower Forest Botanical Gardens, Gun Hill Signal Station or Sunbury Plantation House. These tours can seem rushed, but are fine if you want a drive around the island to see the nicest views and don't want to hire a car. Costs are around US$65-75, children (under 12) half price and include lunch. As well as the Bridgetown Cruise Terminal operators will pick up from south and west coast hotels.

Tour operators also offer more detailed tours to sights, or a combination of places, including Bridgetown and the Garrison, Welchman Hall Gully, Harrison's Cave, St Nicholas Abbey, Hunte's Gardens, Barbados Wildlife Reserve, Bathsheba and the east coast and more. Expect to pay from US$60-80 for a 4-hr tour up to US$100-140 for a full day 7- to 8-hr tour, children (under 12) half price, depending on what the arrangements are; entry fees, distances and whether lunch is included. Explore the tour operator websites for ideas. Another option for a group/family is to charter a vehicle and guide and make up your own itinerary (most tours are by small 8- to 12-seater minibus). Finally, you could also find a taxi driver you like, or get a hotel to recommended one (some of them make very good and entertaining tour guides) and set off on your own; the flat rate is US$32 per hr (many taxis are in fact minibuses).

Andrew Transport, *T822 8007, www.andrewtransportbarbados.com.*
Carson's Taxi & Tour Service, *T240-5339, www.iriebarbadostours.com.*
Coconut Tours, *T437 0297, www.coconutcars.com/Tours.*
Emmanuel Tours, *T824 4254, www.emmanueltoursbarbados.com.*
Glory Tours, *T231 2932, www.glorytours.org.*
Island Safari Barbados, *T429 5337, www.islandsafari.bb.*
Scenic Barbados Tours, *T428 9108, www.scenicbarbadostours.net.*
SunTours Barbados, *T434 8430, www.suntoursbarbados.com.*

Windsurfing and kitesurfing

For the best places to windsurf and kitesurf, see Planning, page 19. Many of the resorts have windsurfing equipment for their guests and staff can provide instruction to get you standing up on a board.

deAction Surf Shop, *Silver Sands, Christ Church, T428 2027, www.briantalma.pro.* Run by Brian Talma, a Barbadian watersports legend, who can rent out boards as well as organize instruction in surfing, windsurfing, kitesurfing and SUPing.

Endless Kiteboarding, *Silver Rock, Christ Church, T420 3253, www.endlesskiteboarding.com.* Run by IKO instructor Roland Boyce, offers 2-hr beginners' lessons from US$120 per person for groups of 2-4, or US$100 per hr for private 1 to 1 instruction. He also offers windsurfing lessons from US$40 per hr and rents out gear.

Background

History

350-1500 The first settlers of the island are believed to be people from mainland South America: the Amerindians (350-650), followed by the Arawak Indians (around 800), and the Caribs who invaded and forced the Arawaks off during the 1200s. The Caribs later left Barbados when the Europeans sailed into the Caribbean region, and by the early 1500s, the island was uninhabited.

1536 Portuguese explorer Pedro a Campos discovered Barbados en route to Brazil. It was Campos who named the island Los Barbados ('the bearded ones'); possibly after the island's fig trees (see box, page 41). The Portuguese didn't stay but left behind some wild pigs, which bred successfully and provided meat for the first English settlers.

1625-1627 Captain John Powell landed on Barbados and claimed the uninhabited island for England. Two years later, his brother Captain Henry Powell landed with a party of 80 settlers and 10 slaves. King Charles I gave the permission to colonize the island, and the group established the island's first European settlement, Jamestown, on the west coast at what is now Holetown.

1639 Governor Henry Hawley founded the House of Assembly. Some 40,000 white settlers (about 1% of the population of England) arrived, mostly small cotton and tobacco farmers.

1643 Commercial production of sugar began, with plants introduced from Brazil by Dutch Jews, who also brought capital, credit, technology and markets.

1651-1652 After the execution of King Charles I (1649), Oliver Cromwell sent a fleet to take over Royalist Barbados but his forces were held at bay for six months. The stalemate with Cromwell was resolved with the signing of the Articles of Agreement, later recognized as the Charter of Barbados by the English Parliament.

1650-1670 A sugar revolution saw the consolidation of land into large estates, marking the end for small farms; most of the original white settlers left. The plantations were owned by the 'landed gentry' who arrived from England, and there was large-scale importation of slave labour from Africa.

1700 By the turn of this century most of the forests had been cleared for sugar, there were more than 800 sugar mills and the population was put at 15,000 whites and 50,000 enslaved blacks.

1751 George Washington visited Barbados; this was his only journey outside the American mainland.

1807 Britain abolished the African slave trade, but not slavery. Barbados exported locally bred slaves to other colonies.

1816 Bussa's Rebellion, when 20,000 slaves from over 70 plantations demonstrated and destroyed sugarcane fields, although no plantation owners or their families died. The uprising was quickly crushed by the West Indian Regiment, and several hundred slaves were killed in battle or hanged afterwards. Signal stations were subsequently built across the island to give advance warning of further rebellions.

1834 The Emancipation Bill was passed by British Parliament with slaves to undergo an apprenticeship period that lasted four years before full emancipation. Men continued to work a 45-hour week without pay in exchange for living in the tiny huts provided by the plantation owners.

1838 Slavery was abolished with full freedom at the end of the apprenticeship period. Barbadian slave owners were compensated with average payments of £20 13s 8d per slave.

1840s Barbadian labourers earned half that of Trinidadians and were the lowest paid in the Caribbean (except Montserrat). Sugar prices fell with greater competition worldwide.

1894 Sugar exports were 50,958 tons, 97% of total exports, but market share was declining because of competition from European sugar beet, while half of all plantations were owned by absentee landlords. Capital investment and technological improvement was minimal.

1898 The Windward Islands Hurricane devastated Barbados, with over 5000 homes completely destroyed, 40,000-45,000 people left homeless, and the sugarcane plantations suffering crippling damage.

1904-1914 About 60,000 workers went to Panama to help construct the canal, 20,000 in 1909 alone.

1923 20,000 migrants left for New York.

1930s Effects of the worldwide depression were felt on Barbados, with unemployment, poor working conditions, falling wages and higher imported food prices. The next events of historical significance involved the advent of labour unions.

1937 Colonial authorities arrested and deported Clement Payne, a trade union organizer from Trinidad who spread word of labour unrest and riots in neighbouring islands and Marcus Garvey's teachings on pan-Africanism. Riots followed, with police shooting and killing 14, wounding 47 and arresting over 400.

1939-1945 The Second World War; there was a reprieve for the sugar industry because of the disruption of beet growing in Europe but U-boat activity limited food imports to the Caribbean islands. The trades union movement continued to gain momentum and the Barbados Labour Party (BLP) was formed, headed by lawyer, Grantley Adams (1898-1971), who had represented Clement Payne in his appeal against deportation.

1945 The West India Royal Commission chaired by Lord Moyne, produced a damning report on neglect and deprivation in the British Caribbean, describing squalid and unhealthy slums and shanty towns and the dire state of education and health provision.

1947 The BLP won the general elections.

1950 Universal adult suffrage was introduced (previously limited only to property owners).

1954 Grantley Adams became the first Premier of Barbados under a new system of ministerial government.

1955 One of the strongest Atlantic hurricanes on record, Hurricane Janet, caused 38 deaths and severe destruction of homes and infrastructure (an estimated US$5 million at the time).

1958-1962 In 1958 all the British Caribbean islands agreed to create the West Indies Federation, with the intention of establishing a political unit that would become independent from Britain as a single state; Grantley Adams served as its first and only premier. Before that could happen, Trinidad and Tobago and Jamaica gained their own independence in 1962 and the federation collapsed. The remaining states once again became self-governing colonies of Britain.

1960s A tourism boom began in Barbados with the introduction of long-haul jet aircraft. But tourism dates right back to the 1700s when such visitors as George Washington came to the island for its healthy environment, and in the 1950s it became a destination for the wealthy, whose lavish lifestyle is still visible primarily along the west coast.

1961 Internal autonomy was granted and Errol Walton Barrow (1920-1987) of the Democratic Labour Party (DLP) replaced Grantley Adams as Premier and the DLP took control of government.

1966 With Barrow at the helm and after several years of peaceful and democratic progress, Barbados became an independent state and formally joined the Commonwealth of Nations on 30 November 1966. Barrow became Barbados' first prime minister, an office he kept until 1976.

1976-present day Since independence, Barbados' politics operate within a framework of a constitutional monarchy (Queen Elizabeth II), and a government of two houses: an elected House of Assembly and an appointed Senate. Power has alternated between the Democratic Labour Party (DLP) and the Barbados Labour Party (BLP). Freundel Stuart of the DLP is currently prime minister, with elections due in February 2018.

Modern Barbados

Barbados won its independence in 1966 after more than three centuries of British rule. In the 18th century, when slavery was at its peak, Africans outnumbered their British masters by three to one. Sugar provided a livelihood for everyone and Barbados was relatively quiet with few slave uprisings. This has been attributed partly to the large military and police presence and the fact that there was nowhere to hide on the small island, but also to slightly better treatment of slaves by their masters than on some other islands. However, resentment grew, particularly after the Haitian Revolution and when emancipation was being debated in England. In 1816 the slaves rose up and burned the cane fields and plantation buildings in a show of defiance – an event still celebrated today.

Slavery was finally abolished in 1838 but not much changed for the blacks. They ended up as very cheap labour and were unable to purchase land of their own. The white plantocracy remained in control of all productive land, becoming allied to a rising merchant class in Bridgetown so as to form an entrenched elite with total financial and political power. Poverty ground down the working class, whether they were black or white (known as redlegs, descended from indentured labourers and deported convicts). Tens of thousands left the country to work on the Panama Canal and those who made money and survived returned to form the nucleus of a black middle class. Resentment

BACKGROUND

Music

No visitor to Barbados can fail to notice the extent to which music pervades daily life. Whether it is reggae pounding out from a passing ZR van or gospel music being belted out in a church, Bajan rhythm is inescapable. The West Africans dragged to the island as slaves brought with them tastes in music and dance which are still evident today. This intensity of sound and beat has produced many musicians, several of which have become world famous, such as The Mighty Gabby, reggae vocalist and songwriter David Kirton, jazz saxophonist Arturo Tappin, Red Plastic Bag and John King, Krosfyah, Square One and Spice. And then there's Rihanna…

Calypso is the musical form for which Barbados is most famous, although it was originally developed in Trinidad. Calypsonians (or kaisonians, as the more historically minded call them) are the commentators, champions and sometime conscience of the people. This unique musical form, a mixture of African, French and, eventually, British, Spanish and even East Indian influences, dates back to Trinidad's first 'shantwell', Gros Jean, late in the 18th century. Since then it has evolved into a popular, potent force, with both men and women (also children, of late) battling for the Calypso Monarch's crown during Crop Over, Barbados' carnival (see box, page 16). The season's calypso songs blast from radio stations and sound systems all over the islands and visitors should ask locals to interpret the sometimes witty and often scurrilous lyrics, for they are a fascinating introduction to the state of the nation. Currently, party soca tunes dominate although some of the commentary calypsonians are still heard on the radio. There is also a new breed of 'Rapso' artists, fusing calypso and rap music. Chutney, an Indian version of calypso, is also becoming increasingly popular and is also being fused with soca, to create 'chutney soca'.

grew again at neglect by Britain, poor wages, poor housing and poor education, and in the 1930s there were riots. Out of conflict, the seeds of a labour movement grew, led by great Barbadians such as Grantley Adams and Errol Walton Barrow (both now National Heroes of Barbados), who went on to found the two main political parties and steer the country to independence.

Just as the political landscape has changed, so there has also been a shift in the economy. Like the other islands just to the west in the Caribbean Sea, sugar is no longer king but has been deposed by tourism. Land formerly devoted to sugarcane has been sold for the construction of resorts and golf courses. While this kind of continual development, which has been going on since the 1960s, is detrimental to the island's ecology and environment (although it was the plantation owners that initially stripped the island of forests and eroded the coastlines), this move to a service economy has been largely successful. Barbados welcomes approximately one million visitors annually (about half of those are cruise passengers), the tourism industry today generates over 50% of the country's foreign exchange and the average Barbadian enjoys one of the highest per capita incomes in the Eastern Caribbean region. It has, however, suffered numerous economic dips because of the general global recession since 2008, particularly from the British holiday market (by far the island's biggest revenue). Nevertheless, holidaymakers

Pan music has a shorter history, developing in the 20th century from the tamboo-bamboo bands which made creative use of tins, dustbins and pans plus lengths of bamboo for percussion instruments. By the end of the Second World War some ingenious souls discovered that huge oil drums could be converted into expressive instruments, their top surfaces tuned to all ranges and depths (eg the ping pong, or soprano pan embraces 28 to 32 notes, including both the diatonic and chromatic scales). Aside from the varied pans, steel bands also include a rhythm section dominated by the steel, or iron men.

Reggae is tremendously popular in Barbados and is played everywhere, all day, all night. However, Barbadians like to vary their reggae so there is also a fusion of reggae and soca, known as ragga-soca, which has a faster rhythm than reggae but slower than up-tempo soca. Ringbang, created in 1994, is a mixture of all the varied types of Caribbean music with the emphasis on the beat rather than the melody.

Tuk is one of the most traditional forms of folk music, having its origins in slave culture of the 17th century, and an important means of expression for the black masses in Barbados. It was banned by the English as subversive; plantation overseers believed that the drums were used to send messages, and it had to wait until after emancipation to resurface officially. Since the revival of Crop Over in 1974, tuk bands have flourished. The instruments used in a tuk band are the kettle drum, bass drum and tin flute. There are several school tuk bands as it is promoted among the younger generation to preserve the island's cultural heritage. The music is lively, with a pulsating rhythm influenced by British regimental band music as well as African dances. It is 'jump-up' music, used at holiday times and carnival for masquerades, when tuk bands travel from village to village, playing popular tunes and inviting audience participation.

go home with nothing but good things to say about the friendliness of Barbadians and the excellent – if sometimes slow (this is the Caribbean after all) – service they received in hotels and restaurants.

Because Barbados lies upwind from the main island arc, it was hard to attack from the sea, so it never changed hands in the colonial wars of the 17th and 18th centuries. There is no French, Dutch or Spanish influence to speak of in the language, cooking or culture. Today, the more obvious outside influences on the Barbadian way of life are North American, from fast-food chains to programmes on television. However, Afro-Caribbean roots are of paramount importance to most Barbadians, reflected in the rhythm of home-grown music and festivals such as Crop Over, as well as food derived from slave rations of staples brought over from Africa.

One withstanding influence from Britain that Barbadians will not shake off though is cricket. In this sport-mad country, everyone has an opinion on the latest matches, the team selection and the state of the West Indies side. In the rare event that you are stuck for a topic of conversation, you can rely on cricket to start a lively debate and a cricket match is symbolic of the way Barbadians approach life – with fun, drama and huge enjoyment in the sport amid a cacophony of noise.

Practicalities

Getting there

Air

Barbados' popularity as a tourist destination has resulted in good flight connections from Europe and North America and you can often pick up good-value deals on package holidays; combining the flight with a hotel can often work out cheaper than booking each separately. Barbados is also the hub of the Eastern Caribbean and has good connections for some island-hopping by air. **Grantley Adams International Airport** ⓘ *www.gaia.bb*, is 16 km from Bridgetown, near the resorts on the south coast and connected to the west coast beaches by the Adams Barrow Cummins (ABC) Highway which bypasses the capital. Flights to Barbados are heavily booked at Christmas and for Crop Over (June-early August).

Flights from the UK

The main scheduled carriers from the UK are **British Airways** ⓘ *www.britishairways.com*, who fly 12 times a week from London Gatwick, and **Virgin Atlantic** ⓘ *www.virgin-atlantic.com*, who fly daily from London Gatwick and weekly from Manchester; both have connecting services to/from mainland Europe. In the winter months (November-April) **Thomas Cook Airlines** ⓘ *www.thomascookairlines.com*, fly from London Gatwick, Manchester, Birmingham and Bristol, and **Thomson** ⓘ *www.thomson.co.uk*, from London Gatwick, Manchester, Birmingham and Glasgow.

> **Tip...**
> Direct flying time to Barbados from UK airports is 7½-9 hours; Miami is 3½ hours; New York five hours; and Toronto four hours.

Flights from the rest of Europe

Condor ⓘ *www.condor.com*, fly seasonally (November-April) three times a week from Frankfurt via either Grenada, St Lucia or Tobago, but most flights from European cities to Barbados connect through the UK. Europeans also have the option of flying with **KLM** or **Air France** to Saint Martin/Sint Maarten, connecting to Barbados with the Caribbean regional airline **LIAT (Leeward Islands Air Transport)** ⓘ *www.liat.com*. Other connecting flights from European cities go via North America; Miami in the US with **American Airlines** or Toronto in Canada with **Air Canada**, for example.

Flights from North America

American Airlines ⓘ *www.aa.com*, fly to Barbados from Miami and Charlotte, **Delta** ⓘ *www.delta.com*, from Atlanta, and **JetBlue** ⓘ *www.jetblue.com*, from New York, Boston and Fort Lauderdale. From Canada, **Air Canada** ⓘ *www.aircanada.com*, fly from Montreal and Toronto, and **WestJet** ⓘ *www.westjet.com*, from Toronto. The other option for North Americans is to fly with **Caribbean Airlines** ⓘ *www.caribbeanairlines.com*, from New York, Orlando, Fort Lauderdale, Miami or Toronto to Trinidad, from where **Caribbean Airlines** or LIAT fly to Barbados.

Flights from South America

LIAT has a direct flight to Barbados from Georgetown in Guyana, and **Avianca** ⓘ *www. avianca.com*, from Bogotá, Colombia; both destinations have other South American connections. **Caribbean Airlines** fly to Barbados via Trinidad from Caracas in Venezuela, Georgetown in Guyana and Paramaribo in Suriname.

Flights from Australia, New Zealand and South Africa
There are no direct flights and connections must be made through North America or London.

Flights from the Caribbean
LIAT connects much of the Caribbean and has direct flights to Barbados from Antigua, Dominica, St Lucia, St Vincent, Grenada, and Trinidad and Tobago, while at their Antigua hub they connect to the Dominican Republic, Puerto Rico, St Thomas, St Croix, Tortola, Anguilla, Saint Martin/Sint Maarten, St Kitts, Nevis and Guadeloupe. From St Lucia you can fly on to Martinique and from Trinidad on to Curaçao. **Caribbean Airlines** connects

> **Tip...**
> Flights on the small airlines between the islands of the Caribbean are generally reliable, but schedules may change and they tend to run on 'island time' (some say LIAT is an acronym for 'Leave Island Any Time'). But this has got its advantages too; they could wait for you if an international connection is delayed.

Barbados to its hubs in Trinidad and Jamaica, from where they connect to other islands: Antigua, Grenada, Nassau, Saint Martin/Sint Maarten, St Lucia and Tobago, as well as their destinations in North and South America. **SVG Air** ⓘ www.flysvgair.com, provides a service between Barbados and St Vincent, and Bequia, Canouan and Union Island in the Grenadines, while **Mustique Airways** ⓘ www.mustique.com, connects Barbados with Mustique in the Grenadines. Private air charter services can be arranged to/from most of the islands with the regional airlines including **LIAT** and **SVG Air** or Barbados-based **Executive Air** ⓘ www.eaairlines.com; for a group taking the maximum number of seats in a small plane seating five to 12, it's worth considering the costs as they can be competitive compared with paying for the same number of scheduled flights.

Airport information
The only airport on the island, **Grantley Adams International Airport** ⓘ Seawell, Christ Church, T428 7101, www.gaia.bb, is modern and well equipped. There are two linked terminals, one for departures and one for arrivals. Facilities include free Wi-Fi, ATMs, foreign exchange bureaux, a post office, car hire agencies (see page 111) in the public area to the left as you exit the arrivals terminal, several food and drinks outlets and quite a wide range of shops including **Cave Sheperd**, an inbound duty-free shop in the arrivals terminal (very useful, saves carrying heavy bottles on the plane).

Taxis stop just outside customs. Check the noticeboard on the left as you come out of arrivals, as it gives the official taxi fares. Alternatively see **www.gaia.bb/content/taxi-rates-airport**. Authorized taxis have a yellow sticker on the side. The taxi dispatcher will give you a trip form and advice on fares; drivers may attempt to charge more if you haven't checked. You can pay in Barbados or US dollars cash. Taxis from the airport to the south coast take 15-30 minutes, to Bridgetown 30 minutes, and to the west coast 40-60 minutes. Example fares are to St Lawrence Gap US$15, Bridgetown US$23, Holetown US$30, and Speightstown US$37.

> **Tip...**
> In a hanger next to the departures terminal is the Barbados Concorde Experience, a museum housing one of these historic and iconic aircraft. On departure, arrive at least an hour earlier at the airport to visit – see page 74.

There is a bus stop on the main road just across the car park, from where large **Transport Board** buses (blue with striped yellow sides) run every 10 minutes along the south coast to Bridgetown, or (over the road) to the Crane. A half-hourly service also goes to Holetown and Speightstown on the west coast. The flat fare is B\$2, and hours of operation are generally 0500-2100. All timetables can be found on the website; **www. transportboard.com**. Very few flights arrive late at night, but if you are delayed, there are hotels a short taxi ride from the airport, see Where to stay, page 84.

Sea

There are no ferry services between Barbados and the other Caribbean islands. Cruise ships call at the **Bridgetown Cruise Terminal** ① *T434 6100, www.barbadosport.com*, and some passengers choose to start, finish or break their cruise in Barbados. The terminal at the **Deep Water Harbour**, about 1.5 km northwest of Bridgetown off Princess Alice Highway, has a **tourist information desk** ① *T426 1718, www.visitbarbados.org, open daily 0900-1700 when cruise ships are in port*, shops, cafés and tour operator desks. Taxis take five minutes to the centre of Bridgetown or it's a 10- to 15-minute walk.

Being on the windward side of the other Lesser Antilles islands, fewer yachts beat their way against the prevailing winds to visit Barbados. Those that do usually arrive after a long passage either from the Canary or Cape Verde islands across the North Atlantic or from Brazil and the South Atlantic. The only cruising area for yachts is along the sheltered west coast; the east coast is rocky and exposed to the Atlantic breakers and should be given a wide berth. The main anchorage is at Carlisle Bay south of Bridgetown, where both the island's two yacht clubs are: **Barbados Yacht Club** and the **Barbados Cruising Club** (see page 38). **Port St Charles** ① *www.portstcharles.com*, is an upscale luxury marina development mainly catering for super yachts near Speightstown on the northwest coast. The two ports of entry for clearing, immigration and customs are the **Bridgetown Deep Water Harbour** and **Port St Charles** ① *open daily 24 hrs (overtime fees applicable 2200-0600), more information from Barbados Port Inc, T434 6100, www.barbadosport.com*. A clearance out certificate from your last port is required. Once you clear into Bridgetown, yachts can go and anchor in Carlisle Bay. But if you want to visit any other areas, including Port St Charles (or Bridgetown and Carlisle Bay from Port St Charles), skippers will need permission from customs and the port authority.

Getting around

Road

At only 34 km long and 22 km wide, the island is fairly small and the terrain is relatively flat, so nowhere takes too long to get to and there's a good choice of transport options. However, away from the main highways on the south and west coasts, the interior rural roads are narrow, winding and poorly signposted, but Barbadians are more than happy to point you in the right direction if you ask. The Adams Barrow Cummins (ABC) Highway cuts inland from the airport to a point between Brighton and Prospect, north of Bridgetown. This road skirts the east edge of the capital, giving access by various roads into the city and to the west and east coasts. Its roundabouts are named after eminent Barbadians, including Sir Garfield Sobers, Errol Barrow and Everton Weekes. The highway and roads into Bridgetown get jammed at rush hour – weekdays 0700-0900 and 1600-1800 – and the city centre is at its worst in the middle of the day. Minibuses and route taxis run around the capital, cheaply and efficiently, but are terribly slow in rush hour when it's often quicker to walk. North of Bridgetown, heading up the west coast, is Highway 1, giving access to all the beach hotels. Highway 2A runs parallel inland, allowing rather speedier access to the north of the island. Along the south coast, Highway 7 runs from the south of Bridgetown and links all the coastal resorts to Oistins.

Bus

The large public buses belonging to the government's **Transport Board** are hard to miss – painted blue with striped yellow sides – and are cheap, frequent and crowded. The flat fare is B$2 per journey anywhere on the island, so if you change

> **Tip...**
> Bus timetables and route finders can be found on the website of the Transport Board: www.transportboard.com.

buses you pay again. The drivers do not have change so exact fare is required; if you are boarding at a terminal, you can get change from the cashier (open 0700-2200). Almost all the routes radiate in and out of Bridgetown, so cross-country journeys are time-consuming if you are staying outside the city centre. However, travelling by bus can be fun. There are some circuits which work quite well; for example: 1) any south coast bus to Oistins, then cross-country bus to the east coast, then direct bus to Bridgetown; 2) any west coast bus to Speightstown, then bus to Bathsheba on the east coast, then direct bus back to Bridgetown. Look out for the red, white and black bus stop signs at the side of the road; out of town bus stops are marked simply 'To City' or 'Out of City'. Some of them have shelters with a bench, and solar USB charging points for phones, but you rarely have to wait too long for a bus on the busier highways.

Around Bridgetown and urban areas, there are plenty of privately owned mid-sized minibuses with B licence plates and painted yellow with blue stripes, and smaller route taxis with ZR licence plates and painted white with maroon stripes. Both typically run shorter routes concentrated in highly trafficked and populated areas. If hailed down, they will usually stop anywhere on their route (though they are not supposed to); travelling by ZR van in particular is quite an experience as they are known for their high speed, loud music, sudden stops and packing in as many passengers as possible. If you feel unsafe then get off and find another – or wait for a blue **Transport Board** bus.

Tip...
If you are moving between hotels on the south coast and the west coast and have luggage, the Transport Board Bridgetown Shuttle runs roughly every hour between the Fairchild Street Terminal and the Princess Alice Terminal and takes about 10-15 minutes; alternatively take a city minibus or taxi.

Buses for the south and east Fairchild Street Terminal for **Transport Board** buses, which is on the south side of the Careenage just over Charles Duncan O'Neal Bridge, and Nursery Drive Minibus and ZR Terminal for other vehicles, which is just across Constitution River from Fairchild Street.

Buses for the west and north Princess Alice Terminal for **Transport Board** buses, which is on Princess Alice Highway on the way to the Deep Water Harbour, and Cheapside Minibus and ZR Terminal for other vehicles, which is to the north on Cheapside. During the rush hour, all these terminals are chaotic, particularly during school term. On most routes, the first buses depart around 0500 and run until at least 2100; on the more popular routes they run until 2400.

Car

Having your own car, if only for a couple days, is highly recommended to get to attractions and restaurants. The network of minor roads criss-crossing the island can be a little confusing and there are plenty of ways to get lost, but Barbados is an enjoyable destination for a bit of a ramble in the interior, distances aren't great, and it won't take long to find the right road again. When all else fails, you can always follow the bus stops saying 'To City' or 'Out of City' (meaning Bridgetown) to help get your bearings. Driving is on the left, and cars are right-hand drive. All passengers must wear seatbelts in the front and back seats, and the use of mobile phones is illegal while driving (except in 'hands-free' mode). The speed limit is 40 or 60 kph depending on the type of road; the ABC Highway and Spring Garden Highway and short sections of Highway 2A have an upper limit of 80 kph. There are plenty of fuel stations in and around Bridgetown, on the main highways and along the west and south coasts; there are fewer on the east coast but distances are very short.

Car hire To hire a car, drivers need to be 21, and those over 70 may require a medical certificate that shows they are fit to drive. You must have a valid (photo) driving license from your own country of residence and a credit card. Car hire is efficient and generally reliable and regular cars, mini mokes, compact SUVs, jeeps and minibuses are all available. Most car rental companies will deliver a vehicle to the airport or your hotel (and can arrange drop-off at a different location for no extra fee), provide a free road map of the island, and will also arrange a local driving permit (mandatory) at a cost of US$5 for two months or US$50 for one year. Many rental companies offer GPS/Sat-Nav systems as well as baby and child booster seats for an extra fee. A medium-sized car or a mini moke will cost on average US$80-100 a day, with discounts for seven or more days. Basic hire generally only includes statutory third-party insurance; you are advised to take out the optional collision damage waiver premium at US$10-12 per day as even the smallest accident can be very expensive. All charges for car hire, excess waiver and other extras are subject to VAT of 17.5%.

Tip...
There are some 60 car hire companies on Barbados but recommended for more than 30 years' experience, good service and island-wide fleet of 300 vehicles is Drive-A-Matic Car Rentals, Grantley Adams International Airport, T434 8440, www.carhire.tv.

Taxi

There are plenty of taxis at the airport, and any hotel and restaurant can phone one. They are unmetered and fares are regulated, but establish what the journey will cost before setting off. At the airport, there is a board displaying the standard taxi fares to various points on the island. Sample fares are US$12 from the airport to Oistins or US$37 from the airport to Speightstown for a car for four people (minibuses are also available). If you find a driver you like, get their card and phone number, and he/she may also offer to be your driver on a tour of the island. Always book ahead if you have a flight to catch.

Essentials A-Z

Accidents and emergencies

Ambulance T511, **Fire** T311, **Police** T211.
Directory assistance T411.

Customs and duty free

Duty-free allowances to Barbados are
1 litre of spirits or wine, 200 cigarettes or
50 cigars, and 60 ml of perfume. Fresh fruit
and vegetables, plants, cuttings and seeds
are restricted or prohibited, depending on
where they've come from, to prevent the
transmission of pests and disease.

Disabled travellers

Wheelchairs are not accommodated on
public road transport and the towns have
very uneven pavements. However, modern
resorts and hotels have rooms with disabled
facilities and it's easy enough to get around
on an organized tour, in a rented vehicle or
by boat, and local people will do their very
best to help.

Drugs

Do not be tempted to dabble in narcotics,
all are illegal and law does not allow for
'personal possession'. Larger amounts of
marijuana or any amount of cocaine will get
you charged with trafficking and penalties
are very severe. If you are offered drugs on
the beach, in a rum shop or at a party, be
warned: some visitors have been found
themselves arrested a few minutes later.

Electricity

110 volts/50 cycles (US standard). Plug types
are 2 flat blades or 2 flat blades with 1 round
grounding pin. Some houses and hotels also
have 240-volt sockets for use with British
equipment or adaptors with 3 rectangular
pins, but take your own, just in case.

Embassies and consulates

For all Barbados embassies and
consulates abroad and for foreign
embassies and consulates in Barbados,
see http://embassy.goabroad.com.

Health

Travel in Barbados poses no health risk to the
average visitor provided sensible precautions
are taken. See your GP or travel clinic at least
6 weeks before departure for general advice
on travel risks and vaccinations. Make sure
you have sufficient medical travel insurance,
get a dental check, know your own blood
group and, if you suffer a long-term
condition such as diabetes or epilepsy, obtain
a **Medic Alert bracelet** (www.medicalert.
org.uk). If you wear glasses, take a copy of
your prescription. No special vaccinations
are required, but a yellow fever inoculation
certificate must be produced on arrival if
you have arrived within 5 days of leaving
an area in Africa or South America affected
with yellow fever.

Insect-borne risks
The major risks posed in the Caribbean
region are those caused by insect disease
carriers such as mosquitoes and sandflies.
The key parasitic and viral diseases are
dengue fever and **chikungunya** (also
known as chik V). Cases of the **Zika virus**,
also spread by mosquitos, have been
reported in the Caribbean from early 2016.
Although the risk of contracting any of
these is very low, it is always a good idea
to protect yourself against mosquitoes; try
to wear clothes that cover arms and legs at
dusk and dawn (when mosquitoes are most
active) and use effective mosquito repellent.
Rooms with a/c or fans also help ward off
mosquitoes at night.

Stomach issues

Some form of diarrhoea or intestinal upset may affect some holidaymakers. The standard advice is always to wash your hands before eating and to be careful with drinking water and ice. Tap water is generally very good, but if in any doubt buy bottled water. Food can also pose a problem; be wary of salads if you don't know whether they have been washed or not. Symptoms should be relatively short lived. Adults can use an antidiarrhoeal medication to control the symptoms but only for up to 24 hrs. In addition, keep well hydrated by drinking plenty of fluids and eat bland foods. Oral rehydration sachets are a useful way to keep well hydrated. These should always be used when treating children and the elderly. If the symptoms persist, consult a doctor.

Sun

The climate is hot, and do not be deceived by cooling sea breezes. Protect yourself adequately against the sun. Apply a high-factor sunscreen (greater than SPF15) and also make sure it screens against UVB. Prevent heat exhaustion and heatstroke by drinking enough fluids throughout the day (your urine will be pale if you are drinking enough). Symptoms of heat exhaustion and heatstroke include dizziness, tiredness and headache. Use rehydration salts mixed with water to replenish fluids and salts and find somewhere cool and shady to recover. If you suspect heatstroke rather than heat exhaustion, you need to cool the body down quickly (cold showers are particularly effective).

If you get sick

There are 2 main hospitals on the island (see below), both in Bridgetown, and both of which offer all services including 24-hr A&E departments and helicopter air-ambulances. As well as hospitals, medical centres and clinics, the larger hotels have doctors on call. For diving emergencies, the hyperbaric chamber is at the **Barbados Defence Force** base on Needham's Point.
Bayview Hospital, St Paul's Av, T436 5446, www.bayviewhospital.com.bb.
Queen Elizabeth Hospital (QEH), Martindale's Rd, T436 6450, www.qehconnect.com.

Useful websites

www.cdc.gov US government site that gives excellent advice on travel health and details of disease outbreaks.
www.fco.gov.uk British Foreign and Commonwealth Office travel site has useful information on each country, people, climate and a list of UK embassies/consulates.
www.fitfortravel.nhs.uk A-Z of vaccine/ health advice for each country.
www.travelhealth.co.uk Independent travel health site with advice on vaccination, travel insurance and health risks.
www.who.int World Health Organization, updates of disease outbreaks.

Insurance

Before departure, it is vital to take out comprehensive travel insurance. There are numerous policies to choose from, so shop around. At the very least, the policy should cover medical expenses, including repatriation to your home country in the event of a medical emergency. Hospital bills need to be paid at the time of admittance, so keep all paperwork to make a claim. There is no substitute for suitable precautions against petty crime, but if you do have something stolen, report the incident to the nearest police station and make sure you get a police report and case number (you will need these to make a claim).

Language

English is the official language although there is a Barbadian dialect spoken, which incorporates West African languages. Barbados uses British spelling of English.

LGBT travellers

Technically same-sex relationships are illegal but laws are rarely enforced and currently under review. There's a relaxed attitude in the tourism industry, although public displays of affection are ill-advised.

Money

US$1 = B$2.00; UK£1 = B$2.59; €1 = B$2.30 (Jun 2017).

The currency is the Barbados dollar, B$, which is pegged at B$2=US$1. Notes are B$2, 5, 10, 20, 50 and 100 and coins are B$1, 25 cents, 10 cents, 5 cents and 1 cent. Many hotel rates, air fares and sometimes activities such as diving and tours quote prices in US dollars, which are widely accepted, although you will get any change in B$.

Changing money

The easiest currencies to exchange are US and Canadian dollars, UK pounds and euros. Credit and debit cards are widely accepted, and if you don't want to carry lots of cash, pre-paid currency cards allow you to pre-load money from your bank account, fixed at the day's exchange rate. They look like a credit or debit card and are issued by specialist money-changing companies, such as **Travelex** and **Caxton FX**. You can top up and check your balance by phone, online and sometimes by text. There are ATMs and foreign exchange bureaux at the airport, and plenty of banks and ATMs in Bridgetown and the other main towns, and ATMs are also found in supermarkets, shopping centres and some fuel stations. Inform your bank before you travel that you are going to Barbados so they don't put a stop on your card. Make sure you bring contact details from home of who to call if your card is lost or stolen.

Opening hours

Banks open Mon-Thu 0800-1500, Fri 0800-1700. Banks at shopping centres are usually open Mon-Thu 1000-1900 and Fri 1000-2000. Some open Sat 1000-1500.

Shops are generally open 0900-1700 Mon-Fri, 0900-1300 Sat, although the larger supermarkets open until at least 1900 and all day on Sun too.

Post and courier services

The **General Post Office** is on Cheapside, Bridgetown, T436 4800, www.barbados postal.com, and there are district post offices in every parish, open Mon 0800-1500 and Tue-Fri 0800-1515. For courier services, **DHL**, www.dhl.com.bb, and **Fedex**, www.fedex. com/bb, cover the island.

Public holidays

1 Jan New Year's Day
21 Jan Errol Barrow Day
Mar/Apr Good Fri, Easter Mon
28 Apr National Heroes' Day
1 May Labour Day
May/Jun Whit Mon
1 Aug Emancipation Day
1st Mon in Aug Kadooment Day
30 Nov Independence Day
25 Dec Christmas Day
26 Dec Boxing Day

Safety

Most visits to Barbados are trouble-free, but there are isolated incidents of crime, including armed robbery, theft from vehicles and sexual assault. But Barbadians are, as a rule, exceptionally friendly, honest and ready to help, and most visitors will not experience any issues and will have a safe and enjoyable stay. The general common-sense rules apply to prevent petty theft: don't exhibit anything valuable and keep wallets and purses out of sight; do not leave your possessions unattended on the beach; use a hotel safe to store valuables, money and passports; lock hotel room doors as noisy fans and a/c can provide cover for sneak thieves; don't leave items on hotel or villa balconies when you go out; at night, avoid deserted areas, including the beaches, and always take taxis. If hiring a car, don't stop if you're flagged down by pedestrians, keep valuables out of sight and lock car doors when driving.

Tax

Departure tax is included in the cost of the air ticket at the point of purchase. 17.5% VAT is included in all prices in shops and restaurants. In hotels, 7.5% VAT and 10% service charge will be added to your bill, usually as a single charge of 17.5%. Check if this has been included in quoted rates. In restaurants, 10% service charge is usually added to the bill, although sometimes for a large group, you are charged 15%.

Telephone and internet

The IDD code for Barbados is +246, followed by a 7-digit number. **Digicel**, www.digicelgroup.com, and **Flow**, www.discoverflow.co, are Caribbean-wide cellular and internet providers. Local SIM cards and start-up packs are available to purchase at phone shops. You'll find these in the major towns, and you can top-up via phone, the websites or buy credit at small shops. Almost all hotels have free Wi-Fi, as well as many restaurants, coffee shops and beach bars.

Time

Atlantic Standard Time, 4 hrs behind GMT, 1 hr ahead of EST.

Tipping

Tipping is not mandatory given that a service charge is added to hotel and restaurant bills and taxi fares are set by the governments and taxi associations. However, given that Barbados receives so many thousands of cruise ship passengers (the majority from the US) a tipping culture is prevalent, so by all means tip if you want to show your appreciation for extra helpful waiting staff in restaurants, a tour guide that has been informative, a taxi driver who has helped with luggage or cleaning staff in hotels. 10% is about right for good service, and it will be most appreciated.

Visas

Visitors must have a passport valid for 6 months after the date of entry and adequate unused pages for stamps. Even though you may not always get asked for it, all travellers need to be able to produce a return or onward ticket, proof that they can support themselves during their stay (a credit card will suffice), and an address at which they will be staying (the hotel on your 1st night should be enough). Most visitors do not need a visa. including citizens of the USA, UK, EU, most Commonwealth countries, South Africa and the Caribbean, although the length of stay permitted varies from 28 days to 6 months. Those in transit or visiting from a cruise ship for less than 24 hrs don't need visas either, even if they are from countries that would otherwise require one. For full details and how to apply for a visa if needed, see the **Ministry of Foreign Affairs and Foreign Trade** website, www.foreign.gov.bb.

State the maximum period you intend to stay on arrival. Overstaying is not recommended if you wish to re-enter Barbados at a later date. Extending your stay is possible by applying to the **Chief Immigration Officer**, Immigration Department, Careenage House on the Wharf in Bridgetown (T434 4100, Mon-Fri 0830-1630); take your passport and return ticket; it's a time-consuming procedure.

Index

*Entries in **bold** refer to maps*

Acknowledgements

Lizzie would like to thank the following for their exceptional help and kind offers of assistance during on-the-ground research for this edition of Barbados: Geeta Chatrani and team at the Yellow Bird Hotel at St Lawrence Gap, Kristin Boland and staff at The Lone Star Hotel and Restaurant, and Sue Jardine and staff at the Coral Reef Club, both on the Platinum Coast, Sandra Edwards at Little Arches and Café Luna at Oistins, and Carrie Walcott at Beach View Barbados at Paynes Bay. For the wheels, thanks to Sueann Griffith and the staff at Drive-A-Matic Car Rentals. Finally, many thanks to all the efficient staff at the tourist offices and outstandingly friendly Caribbean people that helped along the way, to Sarah Cameron for previous editions of the book, and to the team at Footprint for putting it all together.

Credits

Footprint credits
Editor: Felicity Laughton
Production and layout: Emma Bryers
Maps: Kevin Feeney
Colour section: Angus Dawson

Publisher: John Sadler
Head of Publishing: Felicity Laughton
Marketing: Kirsty Holmes
Advertising and Partnerships:
Debbie Wylde

Photography credits
Front cover: shutterstock.com/AlexSt777
Back cover top: shutterstock.com/
Philip Willcocks
Back cover bottom: shutterstock.com/
Anton_Ivanov
Inside front cover: Travel Library Limited/
Superstock.com, Herbert Hopfensperger/
Superstock.com, Axiom Photographic/
Superstock.com.

Colour section
Page 1: Vlad61/Shutterstock.com.
Page 2: Marka/Superstock.com.
Page 4: Filip Fuxa/Shutterstock.com,
shotbydlsamuels/Shutterstock.com.
Page 5: adul24/Shutterstock.com,
age fotostock/Superstock.com,
evenfh/Shutterstock.com.
Page 7: Filip Fuxa/Shutterstock.com,
Susan Seubert/Superstock.com.
Page 8: age fotostock/Shutterstock.com.

Duotone
Page 28: Forcellini Danilo/Shutterstock.com.

Printed in Serbia

Publishing information
Footprint Barbados
3rd edition
© Compass Maps Ltd
October 2017

ISBN: 978 1 911082 24 8
CIP DATA: A catalogue record for this book
is available from the British Library

® Footprint Handbooks and the
Footprint mark are a registered
trademark of Compass Maps Ltd

Published by Footprint
5 Riverside Court
Lower Bristol Road
Bath BA2 3DZ, UK
T +44 (0)1225 469141
footprinttravelguides.com

Every effort has been made to ensure that
the facts in this guidebook are accurate.
However, travellers should still obtain advice
from consulates, airlines, etc about travel
and visa requirements before travelling.
The authors and publishers cannot
accept responsibility for any loss, injury
or inconvenience however caused.